My
iPad® mini

Gary Rosenzweig

que®

800 East 96th Street,
Indianapolis, Indiana 46240 USA

My iPad® mini

Copyright © 2013 by Pearson Education, Inc.

ISBN-13: 978-0-7897-4876-8
ISBN-10: 0-7897-4876-2

Library of Congress Cataloging-in-Publication Data is on file and available upon request.

Printed in the United States of America

Second Printing: February 2013

Trademarks

Warning and Disclaimer

Bulk Sales

Que Publishing offers excellent discounts on this book when ordered in quantity for bulk purchases or special sales. For more information, please contact

U.S. Corporate and Government Sales
1-800-382-3419
corpsales@pearsontechgroup.com

For sales outside of the U.S., please contact

International Sales
international@pearsoned.com

EDITOR-IN-CHIEF
Greg Wiegand

ACQUISITIONS EDITOR
Laura Norman

MANAGING EDITOR
Kristy Hart

PROJECT EDITOR
Lori Lyons

SENIOR INDEXER
Cheryl Lenser

EDITORIAL ASSISTANT
Cindy Teeters

BOOK DESIGNER
Anne Jones

COMPOSITOR
Bronkella Publishing

Contents at a Glance

Table of Contents

About the Author

Gary Rosenzweig is an Internet entrepreneur, software developer, and technology writer. He runs CleverMedia, Inc., which produces websites, computer games, apps, and podcasts.

CleverMedia's largest site, MacMost.com, features video tutorials for Apple enthusiasts. It includes many videos on using Macs, iPhones, and iPads.

Gary has written numerous computer books, including *ActionScript 3.0 Game Programming University*, *MacMost.com Guide to Switching to the Mac*, *Special Edition Using Director MX*, *My Pages (for Mac)*, and *My iPad, Fifth Edition*.

Gary lives in Denver, Colorado, with his wife, Debby, and daughter, Luna. He has a computer science degree from Drexel University and a master's degree in journalism from the University of North Carolina at Chapel Hill.

Website: http://garyrosenzweig.com

Twitter: http://twitter.com/rosenz

More iPad Tutorials and Book Updates: http://macmost.com/ipadguide/

Acknowledgments

Thanks, as always, to my wife, Debby, and my daughter, Luna. Also thanks to the rest of my family: Jacqueline Rosenzweig, Jerry Rosenzweig, Larry Rosenzweig, Tara Rosenzweig, Rebecca Jacob, Barbara Shifrin, Richard Shifrin, Barbara H. Shifrin, Tage Thomsen, Anne Thomsen, Andrea Thomsen, and Sami Balestri.

Thanks to all the people who watch the show and participate at the MacMost website.

Thanks to everyone at Pearson Education who worked on this book: Laura Norman, Lori Lyons, Tricia Bronkella, Kathy Ruiz, Kristy Hart, Cindy Teeters, Anne Jones, and Greg Wiegand.

We Want to Hear from You!

As the reader of this book, *you* are our most important critic and commentator. We value your opinion and want to know what we're doing right, what we could do better, what areas you'd like to see us publish in, and any other words of wisdom you're willing to pass our way.

As an Editor-in-Chief for Que Publishing, I welcome your comments. You can email or write me directly to let me know what you did or didn't like about this book—as well as what we can do to make our books better.

Please note that I cannot help you with technical problems related to the topic of this book. We do have a User Services group, however, where I will forward specific technical questions related to the book.

When you write, please be sure to include this book's title and author as well as your name, email address, and phone number. I will carefully review your comments and share them with the author and editors who worked on the book.

Email: feedback@quepublishing.com

Mail: Que Publishing
            ATTN: Reader Feedback
            800 East 96th Street
            Indianapolis, IN 46240 USA

Reader Services

Visit our website and register this book at quepublishing.com/register for convenient access to any updates, downloads, or errata that might be available for this book.

Learn to tap, swipe, flick, and pinch your way through the iPad's interface.

Learn to use the iPad's physical switches.

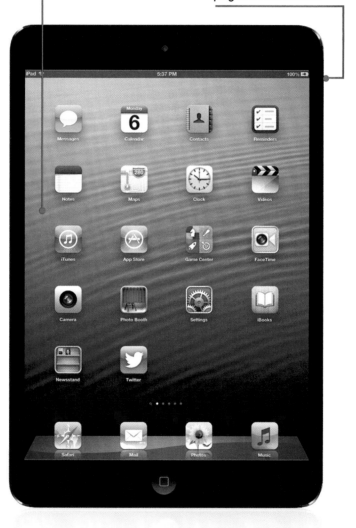

In this chapter, you learn how to perform specific tasks on your iPad to become familiar with the interface.

→ The Evolving iPad

→ The iPad mini's Buttons and Switches

→ Screen Gestures

→ iPad mini Screens

→ Interacting with Your iPad mini

→ Using Siri

Getting Started

Before you learn how to perform specific tasks on your iPad mini, you should become familiar with the interface. If you have used an iPhone or iPod touch, you already know the basics. But if the iPad mini is your first touch-screen device, you need to take time to become accustomed to interacting with it.

The Evolving iPad

There have been several generations of iPads, each adding new features and capabilities. They are very similar, and the more recent models can all run the same OS and apps. It is useful to know how your iPad mini compares to the rest of the product line.

Generations of iPads

The following table shows the major differences between these iPads:

IPAD COMPARISON CHART

	iPad	iPad 2	3rd Generation	4th Generation	iPad mini
Released	April 2010	March 2011	March 2012	November 2012	November 2012
Weight	1.5 lbs/700g	1.3 lbs/600g	1.4 lbs/650g	1.4 lbs/650g	.7 lbs/300g
Thickness	.53 inches	.34 inches	.37 inches	.37 inches	.28 inches
Display diagonal size	9.7-inch	9.7-inch	9.7-inch	9.7-inch	7.9-inch
Screen resolution	768x1024	768x1024	1536x2048 Retina	1536x2048 Retina	768x1024
Front-facing camera	None	0.3MP/VGA	0.3MP/VGA	1.2MP/720p HD	1.2MP/720p HD
Rear-facing camera	None	0.7MP/720p	5MP/1080p	5MP/1080p	5MP/1080p
Processor	A4	A5	A5X	A6X	A5
Dock connector	30-pin	30-pin	30-pin	Lightning	Lightning
Siri-compatible			✓	✓	✓

	iPad	iPad 2	3rd Generation	4th Generation	iPad mini
Optional mobile connection	2G/3G	2G/3G	2G/3G/4G	2G/3G/4G	2G/3G/4G
iOS 6-compatible		✓	✓	✓	✓

All iPads have a screen that uses a 3 by 4 ratio. They all behave like the screen is 768 by 1024 pixels, like the iPad, iPad 2, and your iPad mini. Some iPads, the 3rd and 4th generations, have a retina display that is actually 1536 by 2048 pixels. They still display the same amount of content that your iPad mini does, but they show more detail in photographs, text, and graphics.

Another difference between iPads is the cameras. The original iPad had no camera at all. The 2nd and 3rd generations had cameras, but the more recent iPads, including the iPad mini, have a rear-facing camera that is capable of much higher resolution for both still photos and video.

Each iPad has also become a little more powerful with a faster processor at its heart. The iPad mini has the dual-core A5 processor, which gives it the capability to handle voice dictation and render beautiful graphics for games.

iOS 6

The primary piece of software on the iPad is the operating system, known as iOS. This is what you see when you flip through the screens of icons on your iPad and access the various default apps such as Mail, Safari, Photos, and iTunes.

This book covers iOS 6.0, the version released in September 2012. There have been six generations of the software that runs iPhones and iPads. The original iPhone OS was developed for the first iPhone. The third version, iOS 3, worked on iPhones and the iPad. This latest version, iOS 6, works on the iPad 2 and newer devices, including the iPad mini.

The iPad mini's Buttons and Switches

The iPad features a Home button, a Wake/Sleep button, a volume control, and side switch.

The Home Button

The Home button is probably the most important physical control on the iPad and the one that you will use the most often. Pressing the Home button returns you to the Home screen of the iPad when you are inside an application, such as Safari or Mail, and you want to get back to your Home screen to launch another app. You can also double press the Home button to see icons for your other applications and controls for audio or video playback, without leaving the current application.

Where's the Quit Button?
Few, if any, apps on the iPad have a way to quit. Instead, think of the Home button as the Quit button. It closes out the current app and returns you to your Home screen. The app is actually still running, but paused, in the background. To completely quit an app, see "Quitting Apps," in Chapter 15.

The Wake/Sleep Button

The primary function of the Wake/Sleep button (sometimes called the On/Off button) at the top of your iPad is to quickly put it to sleep. Sleeping is different than shutting down. When your iPad is in sleep mode, you can instantly wake it to use it. You can wake up from sleep by pressing the Wake/Sleep button again or pressing the Home button.

Peek a Boo!

If you are using the Apple iPad mini Smart Cover (see Chapter 18), your iPad will go to sleep when you close it and wake up when you open it, as long as you use the default settings.

The Wake/Sleep button can also be used to shut down your iPad, which you might want to do if you leave your iPad for a long time and want to preserve the battery life. Press and hold the Wake/Sleep button for a few seconds, and the iPad begins to shut down and turn off. Confirm your decision to shut down your iPad using the Slide to Power Off button on the screen.

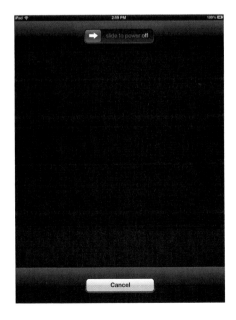

To start up your iPad, press and hold the Wake/Sleep button for a few seconds until you see something appear on the screen.

When Should I Turn Off My iPad mini?

It is normal to never turn off your iPad. In sleep mode, with the screen off, it uses little power. If you plug it in to power at night or during longer periods when you aren't carrying it with you, you don't need to ever shut it down.

The Volume Control

The volume control on the side of your iPad mini is actually two buttons: one to turn the volume up, and the other to turn it down.

Your iPad keeps two separate volume settings in memory: one for head-phones and one for the internal speakers. If you turn down the volume when using headphones and then unplug the headphones, the volume changes to reflect the last settings used when headphones were not plugged in and vice versa. A Speaker icon and a series of rectangles display on the screen to indicate the level of volume.

The Side Switch

The switch on the side of your iPad can do one of two things: It can be set as a mute switch or an orientation lock. You can decide which function this button performs in your iPad's settings. See "Setting Side Switch Functionality" in Chapter 2.

If you choose to use this switch as a mute switch, it will mute all sound if switched to the off position. You will see a speaker icon appear briefly in the middle of the screen when you do this. A line through the icon means you just muted the sound; otherwise, you just unmuted your iPad. By default, the iPad mini comes with the switch configured to mute.

If you choose to use this switch as an orientation lock, it will do something else entirely. Your iPad has two primary screen modes: vertical and horizontal. You can use almost every default app in either orientation. For example, if you find that a web page is too wide to fit on the screen in vertical orientation, you can turn the iPad sideways and the view changes to a horizontal orientation.

When you don't want your iPad to react to its orientation, slide the iPad side switch so that you can see the orange dot, which prevents the orientation from changing. When you need to unlock it, just slide the lock off.

This comes in handy in many situations. For instance, if you are reading an ebook in bed or on a sofa while lying on your side, then you may want vertical orientation even though the iPad is lying sideways.

Orientation and Movement

I know I said there were only four physical switches on your iPad, but there is another one: the entire iPad.

Your iPad knows which way it is oriented, and it knows if it is being moved. The simplest indication of this is that it knows whether you hold it vertically with the Home button at the bottom or horizontally with the Home button to one of the sides. Some apps, especially games, use the exact screen orientation of the iPad to guide screen elements and views.

Shake It Up!
One interesting physical gesture you might perform is the "shake." Because your iPad can sense movement, it can sense when you shake it. Many apps take advantage of this feature and use it to set off an action, such as shuffling songs in the Music app or erasing a drawing canvas.

Screen Gestures

Who knew just a few years ago that we'd be controlling computing devices with taps, pinches, and flicks rather than drags, key presses, and clicks? Multitouch devices such as the iPhone, iPod Touch, and the iPad have added a new vocabulary to human-computer interaction.

Tapping and Touching

Since there is no mouse, a touch screen has no cursor. When your finger is not on the screen, there is no arrow pointing to anything.

A single, quick touch on the screen is usually called a "tap" or a "touch." You usually tap an object on the screen to perform an action.

Occasionally you need to double-tap—two quick taps in the same location. For instance, double-tapping an image on a web page zooms in to the image. Another double-tap zooms back out.

Pinching

The screen on the iPad is a multitouch screen, which means it can detect more than one touch at the same time. This capability is used all the time with the pinch gesture.

A pinch (or a pinch in) is when you touch the screen with both your thumb and index finger and move them toward each other in a pinching motion. You can also pinch in reverse, which is sometimes called an "unpinch" or "pinch out."

An example of when you would use a pinch would be to zoom in and out on a web page or photograph.

Dragging and Flicking

If you touch the screen and hold your finger down, you can drag it in any direction along the screen. This action often has the effect of moving the content on the screen.

For instance, if you are viewing a long web page and drag up or down, the page will scroll. Sometimes an app will let you drag content left and right as well.

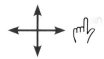

What if you have a long web page or a list of items inside an app? Instead of dragging the length of the screen, lifting your finger up, and moving it to the bottom to drag again, you can "flick." Flicking is like dragging, but you move quickly and lift your finger off the screen at the last moment so that the content continues to scroll after you have lifted your finger. You can wait for it to stop scrolling or touch the screen to make it stop.

Pull Down and Release Update

A common gesture is to tap in a list of items, drag down, and release. For instance, you would do this in Mail to get new messages. You would also do this in Twitter to get new tweets. Many Apple and third-party apps use this gesture to let you signal that you want to update the list of items. So if you don't see an obvious "update now" button, try this gesture.

Four-Finger Gestures

You can perform one of three special functions by using four or five fingers at a time on the screen. If you put four or five fingers on the screen and pinch them all together, you will be taken out of your current app and back to the Home screen, similar to just pressing the Home button.

You can swipe left or right using four or more fingers to quickly page between running apps without going to the Home screen first. Swiping up with four fingers will bring you to the multitask switcher. See "Viewing Currently Running Apps" in Chapter 15.

iPad mini Screens

Unlike a computer, the iPad screen does only one thing at a time. Let's go through some of the typical screens you see while getting to know your iPad.

The Lock Screen

The default state of your iPad when you are not using it is the lock screen. This is just a picture with the time at the top and a large slider at the bottom with the words "slide to unlock" and single button to the right of the slider for launching a picture frame photo slideshow (see Chapter 9).

By default, you see the lock screen when you wake up your iPad. Sliding the unlock slider takes you to the Home screen or to whichever app you were using when you put the iPad to sleep.

The Home Screen

Think of the Home screen as a single screen but with multiple pages that each features different app icons. At the bottom of the Home screen are app icons that do not change from page to page. The area resembles the Mac OS X Dock.

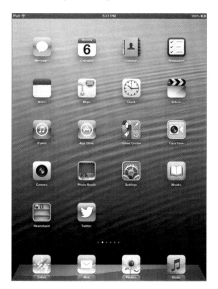

The number of pages on your Home screen depends on how many apps you have. The number of pages you have is indicated by the white dots near the bottom of the screen, just above the bottom icons. The brightest dot represents the page you are currently viewing. You can move between pages on your Home screen by dragging or flicking left or right.

To the left of the dots is a small magnifying glass that represents the search screen. We talk about that in a minute.

An App Screen

When you tap on an app icon on the Home screen, you run that app just like you would run an application on your computer. The app takes over the entire screen.

At this point, your screen can look like anything. If you run Safari, for instance, a web page displays. If you run Mail, you see a list of your new email or a single incoming email message.

The Search Screen

If you are on your Home screen, looking at page one of your app icons, you can drag to the right to get to the Search screen, which has a Search iPad field at the top and a keyboard at the bottom.

You can type in anything to search for a contact, app, email message, photo, and so on. You don't have to define what type of thing you want to search for.

1. From the Home screen, drag left to right to go to the Search screen.

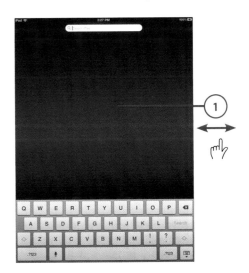

2. Type a search term using the on-screen keyboard.

3. You see a list of items on your iPad that match the search term. Tap the Search button on the keyboard to dismiss the keyboard and complete the search.

4. Tap the X in the search field to clear the search and start again.

5. Tap any of the items to go to the appropriate app and view the content.

The Settings Screen

One of the apps that you have on your iPad by default is the Settings app. With the Settings app, you can control several basic preferences for your iPad. (See Chapter 2 for more on customizing settings.)

This is really just another app screen, but it is worth singling out as you'll need it to customize most aspects of your iPad.

Interacting with Your iPad mini

Now let's examine the different types of on-screen interface elements, the on-screen keyboard and how to use it, and specialized interactions such as text editing and copy and paste.

Common Interface Elements

Several interface elements are more complex than a simple button. In typical Apple style, these elements are often self-explanatory, but if you have never used an iPhone or iPod touch before, you might find some that give you pause.

Sliders

A slider is really just a button. But instead of tapping it, you need to tap and drag to the right to indicate that you want to perform the action, which makes it harder to accidentally trigger the action.

The most obvious example is the slider at the bottom of the Lock screen. If there were a button there, it might be too easy to unlock your iPad without realizing it.

Switches

A switch is also like a simple button, but you need to tap only the switch to activate it. A switch gives you feedback about which state it is in.

For example, switches indicate whether the Sound Check and Lyrics & Podcast Info features of the Music app are on or off. Tapping on either switch changes the position of the switch.

Sound Check	OFF
EQ	Off >
Volume Limit	Off >
Group By Album Artist	ON

Toolbars

Some apps have a set of buttons in a toolbar at the top of the screen that are general controls. The toolbar might disappear or the buttons might vary depending on the mode of the app. An example of a toolbar is in the iTunes app.

Menus

Often tapping a single button in a toolbar brings up more buttons or a list of choices, which are like menus on your Mac or PC. The choices in the list are usually related. For example, a button in Safari gives you many different ways to share a web page.

Tab Bars

Sometimes you see a row of buttons at the bottom of the screen that function similarly to toolbars, but each button represents a different mode for the app. For instance, at the bottom of the App Store app, you see a Tab bar that you use to switch between various lists of apps: Featured, Top Charts, Genius, Purchased, and Updates.

Using the On-Screen Keyboard

The interface element you might interact with the most is the on-screen keyboard. It pops up from the bottom of the screen automatically whenever you need to enter some text.

The default keyboard has only letters and the most basic punctuation available. There are two shift keys that enable you to enter uppercase letters. You also have a Backspace key and a Return key.

Is There a Quicker Way to Capitalize?

So to capitalize a word, you tap the Shift key and then type the letter, right? You can. But a faster way is to tap the Shift key; then, without letting your finger off the screen, drag it to the letter and release in a single tap, slide, release action.

You can do the same with numbers and punctuation by tapping the .?123 key and sliding and releasing over the key you want.

To enter numbers and some other punctuation, tap the .?123 key to switch your keyboard into a second mode for numbers and punctuation.

To return to the letters, just tap the ABC key, or tap the #+= key to go to a third keyboard that includes less frequently used punctuation and symbols.

There are other keyboard variations. For instance, if you type in a location that needs a web address, a keyboard that doesn't have a spacebar appears that instead has commonly used symbols such as colons, slashes, underscores, and even a .com button. Instead of a Return key, you might see an action word like "Search" written on that key—tapping it will perform an action like searching the web. All keyboards include a button at the bottom right that enables you to hide the keyboard if you want to dismiss it.

You can also split the keyboard and/or move it up away from the bottom of the screen. Just tap and hold the keyboard button at the bottom-right corner of the keyboard. It has a little keyboard icon on it. Then select Undock or Split. The first will simply move the keyboard to the middle of the screen. The second will do that as well, but will also split the keyboard into two halves. You can then drag the keyboard up and down by tapping, holding, and dragging on that same keyboard button. Drag it all the way back down to the bottom to dock it to the bottom again. You can also split the keyboard by placing two fingers on the keyboard and dragging them apart, and then rejoin it by dragging the fingers together.

Dictating Text

If you have a 3rd generation iPad you can also dictate text using your voice rather than typing on the keyboard. Almost any time you see a keyboard you should also see a small microphone button to the left of the spacebar. Tap that and you will be prompted to speak to your iPad.

1. Any time you see the default keyboard, you will see the microphone button to the left

of the spacebar. Tap it to begin dictating.

2. A larger button will spring from the smaller dictation button. The purple color filling the microphone will measure the volume of your voice. When you are done dictating, tap this larger button to end the dictation.

3. After you tap the larger button it will disappear and three dots will appear in place of your text cursor and pulse while your iPad transcribes the audio to text. Simply wait for the transcription to complete.

Talk somewhat slowly and clearly, and in segments about the length of a sentence for best results. Of course this feature isn't perfect. Pay careful attention to what is transcribed and correct any mistakes using the keyboard. Over time you will get better at speaking in a way that minimizes mistakes.

DICTATION TIPS

The dictation button will appear any time a standard keyboard is present in any app. You can use it in Notes, Pages, or any writing app. You can use it in search fields and text entry fields on the web. But you cannot use it when there are specialty keyboards like the ones used to enter in email addresses, web URLs, telephone numbers, and so on. So, for instance, you can use it in Safari to type in the search field, but not the web address field.

You need to be connected to the Internet for dictation to work. Your iPad sends the audio to Apple's servers, which handle the transcription and send the text back to your iPad. If you are not connected, it won't work.

Dictation works according to your language set in Settings, General, Keyboard, International Keyboards. Not all languages are supported, but Apple is adding more all the time.

You can indicate the end of a sentence by saying "period" or "question mark." You can also speak other punctuation like "comma" or "quote."

You can also speak commands like "new line" or "cap" to capitalize the next word. There is no official list of what the dictation feature supports, and since the transcription takes place on Apple's servers they can change how it handles commands at any time.

Editing Text

Editing text has its challenges on a touch-screen device. Even though you can just touch any portion of your text on screen, your finger tip is too large for the level of precision you usually get with a computer mouse and cursor. To compensate, Apple developed an editing technique using a magnifying glass area of the screen that you get when you touch and hold over a piece of text.

For example, if you want to enter some text into a field in Safari, touch and hold on the field. A circle of magnification appears with a cursor placed at the exact location you selected.

When you find the exact location that you want to indicate, release your finger from the screen. Then a variety of options display, depending on what kind of text you selected, such as Select, Select All, and Paste. You can ignore the options presented and start typing again to insert text at this location.

Copy and Paste

You can copy and paste text inside an app, and between apps, on your iPad. Here's how you might copy a piece of text from one document to another in the Notes app.

1. Launch Notes. If you don't have any notes yet, create one by typing some sample text.

2. Touch and hold over a word in your note. The Select/Select All pop-up menu appears.

3. Choose Select.

4. Some text appears highlighted surrounded by dots connected to lines. Tap and drag the dots so the highlighted area is exactly what you want.

5. Tap Copy.

6. Tap the + button to create a new note.

7. Tap the empty document area once to bring up a pop-up menu with the Paste command.

8. Tap Paste to insert the copied text.

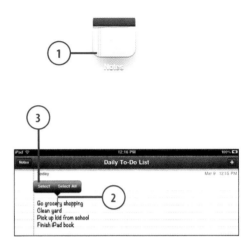

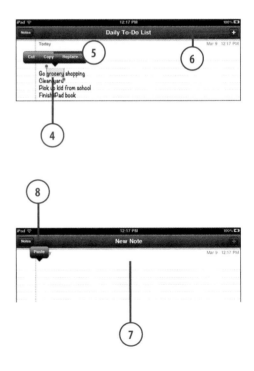

Using Siri

Siri is a voice-activated assistant that was first introduced in 2011 on the iPhone 4S. You can use your voice and speak commands to your iPhone and Siri will respond. It will either give you information or take action using one of the apps on the iPhone.

You can also use Siri on your iPad mini. First, you need to make sure you have Siri turned on. Then, you use the Home button to activate Siri.

1. In your Settings app, tap the General settings.

2. Then tap Siri.

3. Slide the switch to ON to enable Siri.

4. Press the Home button to exit Settings.

5. Press and hold the Home button for about a second. The Siri interface will pop up, showing a microphone button with a purple light that changes as you speak.

Settings		General
Airplane Mode	OFF	
Wi-Fi	CleverMedia	About >
Bluetooth	On	Software Update >
Do Not Disturb	OFF	Usage >
Notifications		Siri >
General		VPN Not Connected >
Sounds		iTunes Wi-Fi Sync >
Brightness & Wallpaper		

1   **2**   **3**

General   **Siri**

Siri   ON

Siri helps you get things done just by asking. You can make a FaceTime call, send a message, dictate a note, or even find a restaurant.

About Siri and Privacy

Language   English (United States) >

Voice Feedback   Always >

My Info   None >

To talk to Siri, press and hold the home button and speak.

5

What can I help you with?   i

Mail   Photos

6. Speak clearly at a normal pace and say "How's the weather outside?" After a short delay, the words you spoke will appear and Siri will attempt to perform an action based on those words.

7. In this case, a short weather forecast will appear.

8. Siri also responds with a statement and will speak it audibly. The text of the response will typically appear above the response.

SIRI TIPS

To use Siri, you must have a connection to the Internet. It can be a Wi-Fi connection or a mobile connection. When you speak text, the audio is transmitted to Apple's servers to convert it to text and interpret the command. The results are sent back to your iPad.

It is best to speak clearly and to limit background noise. Using Siri in a quiet room works better than in a crowded outdoor space or in a car with the radio on, for instance.

Because Apple's servers control Siri, they can update Siri's capabilities at any time. So right now Siri may not understand your request for local sports scores, but in the future you might try it and find out it works.

You can use Siri to perform many tasks on your iPad without typing. For example, you can search the Web, set reminders, send messages, and play music. Throughout the rest of this book, look for the Siri icon for tips on how to use Siri to perform a task related to that section of the book.

Customize how your iPad looks and works
through the Settings app.

In this chapter, you learn how to change some of the settings on your iPad such as your background images, sounds, password, and how some apps behave.

Customizing Your iPad

Like with any relationship, you fall in love with your iPad for what it is. And then, almost immediately, you try to change it.

It's easier, though, to customize your iPad than it is your significant other because you can modify various settings and controls in the Settings app. You can also move icons around on the Home screen and even change how the Home button works.

Changing Your Wallpaper

The wallpaper is the image behind the icons on the Home screen and on the lock screen, so make sure it's something you like.

1. Tap the Settings icon on your Home screen.

2. Choose Brightness & Wallpaper from the Settings on the left side of the screen.

3. Tap the Large Wallpaper button that shows previews of your lock and home screens.

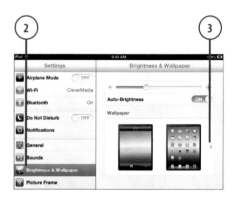

4. If you haven't yet loaded or taken any pictures on to your iPad, you'll move right to step 5. Otherwise, to choose an Apple-supplied wallpaper, tap Wallpaper or choose a photo album and skip ahead to step 11.

5. Tap an image icon to select it. You see a full view of the image.

6. From this full view, choose Set Lock Screen to set this image as the background of your lock screen.

7. Choose Set Home Screen to set this image as the background for your Home screen.

8. Choose Set Both to make the image the background for both screens.

9. Tap Cancel at the upper-left corner of the screen to go back to the wallpaper icons.

10. When viewing the list of icons, tap the Back button at the top of the screen to go back to the previous screen.

11. Tap Photo Library or a photo album to view your photos.

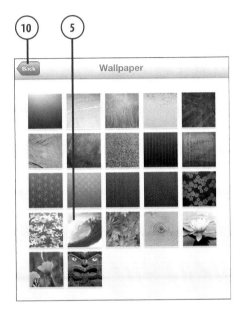

12. Tap a photo icon to view that photo from your photo album.

13. Use the buttons described in steps 6, 7, and 8 to set this image as a background.

Adjusting the Wallpaper Image

You can touch and drag in a photo to move to other areas of the image so you can choose the part of the image you want as your wallpaper. You can also pinch to zoom in and out on your photographs.

Getting Details About Your iPad

One of the many things in the Settings app on the iPad is an About section, from which you can learn details about your iPad.

1. Tap the Settings icon on your Home screen.

2. Tap General from the list of settings on the left.

3. Tap About, the first button at the top of the list of General settings.

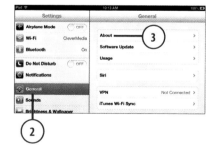

4. See how many songs, videos, photos, and apps you have.

5. See the total capacity of your iPad and the amount of space available.

Why Am I Missing Space?

Notice in the example here that the capacity of the iPad is shown as 13.4GB. However, that particular model is advertised as a "16GB" model. The discrepancy between the two is because of space used by the operating system and other system files.

General	About	
Name	iPad mini >	**9**
Songs	0	
Videos	0	
Photos	113	
Applications	18	**4**
Capacity	13.7 GB	
Available	11.0 GB	**5**
Version	**6** 6.0.1 (10A523)	
Model	MD528LL	**7**
Serial Number	F4GJKC0TF193	
Wi-Fi Address	E4:8B:7F:A0:4F:93	**8**
Bluetooth	E4:8B:7F:A0:4F:94	

6. The version number tells you which version of the iPad operating system you are running. Check this to make sure you are running the latest version of the iPad OS.

7. The model number tells you exactly which iPad you own if you happen to get it serviced or perhaps to report a bug to a third-party app developer.

8. The serial number, Wi-Fi address, and Bluetooth address are unique to your iPad. Apple may ask for your serial number if you are sending your iPad in for repairs. The Wi-Fi number is what you need if you are asked for a "MAC address" or "Ethernet address" for your iPad.

9. You can change the name of your iPad as it is seen in iTunes and iPhoto when you sync with your computer and various other instances.

Another Model Number?

If you tap the Legal button and the Regulatory button on the About screen, you are taken to another screen that lists another model number for your iPad. For the iPad mini, Wi-Fi only model, this is A1432. When you are buying third-party accessories for your iPad, the specifications for those accessories may say "compatible with model X." In that case, X may represent either model number.

Setting Alert Sounds

Your iPad can be a noisy device with various events that trigger alert sounds. Just typing on the on-screen keyboard can produce a series of clicks.

Here's how to adjust your iPad's alert sounds.

1. Tap the Settings icon on the Home screen.

2. Tap Sounds from the list of settings on the left.

3. The volume slider is a separate control for incoming call rings from FaceTime.

4. When Change with Buttons is turned off, the ringer volume (see step 3) and alert volume (side volume buttons) are separate. When you turn this on, they are locked to the same setting, and you can use the slider to adjust both.

5. Tap any of these settings to set the sound that plays when an event occurs. You can choose ringtones, alert tones, or custom tones for any of the events. Ringtones refers to FaceTime calls and Text Tones refers to the Messages app.

6. Switch the Lock Sounds on or off. When this setting is on, a sound plays when you unlock the Lock screen.

7. Switch Keyboard Clicks on or off.

How About Custom Sounds?

Any sound event can play a ringtone rather than a plain alert sound. You will see a list of "Alert Tones" that are built into iOS, as well as a list of ringtones, which include the built-in ringtones and any custom ringtones. You can add your own custom ringtones in iTunes on your Mac or PC and then sync them with your iPad. After the sync, you will see them listed when selecting an alert sound. See "Syncing Music," in Chapter 3. By obtaining or creating your own custom ringtones, you can set your alert sounds to anything you want.

Password Protecting Your iPad

Password protecting your iPad is a great way to make sure that someone else can't access your information or use your iPad.

1. Tap the Settings icon on the Home screen.

2. Tap General from the list of settings on the left.

3. Tap Passcode Lock.

Even More Security

To lock your iPad automatically when you aren't using it, choose Auto-Lock from the General Settings and set your iPad to automatically lock at 2, 5, 10, or 15 minutes. You can also choose to never have it auto-lock. Of course, you can manually lock your iPad at any time by pressing the Wake/Sleep button at the top.

4. Tap Simple Passcode to switch from using a 4-digit number to a longer password that can include both letters and numbers, if you want additional security; otherwise, your password will consist of 4 digits. Tap Turn Passcode On.

5. Type in a four-digit passcode that you can easily remember. Write it down and store it in a safe place as you can run into a lot of trouble if you forget it.

6. You will be asked to re-enter your passcode.

7. Tap the Require Passcode button and choose the delay before a passcode is required. If you choose anything other than Immediately, then someone else using your iPad can work on it for that period of time before needing to enter the code.

8. Turn off Picture Frame to remove the Picture Frame slideshow button on the Lock screen.

9. Turn off Siri to disable the ability to use Siri from the Lock screen.

10. Turn on Erase Data if you want to erase the iPad data after 10 failed passcode attempts.

11. Press the Wake/Sleep button to confirm your new settings work. Then press the Home button and Slide to Unlock. The Enter Passcode screen displays.

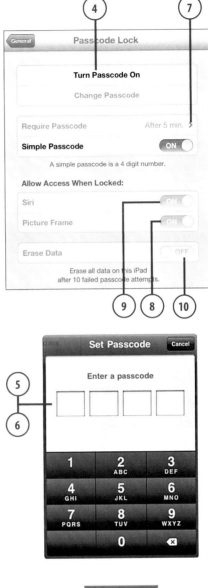

You Forgot Your Passcode?

Well, it wouldn't be secure if there were a way to get around the passcode, so you're out of luck until you can connect your iPad to your Mac or PC and use iTunes to restore it. Hopefully, this never happens to you.

Setting Parental Restrictions

If you plan to let your kids play with your iPad, you might want to set some restrictions on what they can do.

1. Tap the Settings icon on the Home screen.

2. Tap General.

3. Tap Restrictions.

4. Tap Enable Restrictions to turn restrictions on or tap Disable Restrictions to turn them off.

5. Type in a four-digit code and then re-enter the code when prompted. Remember this code, or you can't turn off restrictions.

6. To remove the Safari, Camera, FaceTime, and iTunes apps from your Home screen, turn the switches to off.

7. The Installing Apps switch prevents new apps from being installed.

8. The Location switch turns off location-based functions of all apps.

9. You can disallow adding or changing email accounts.

10. Pick which country's rating system to use from the Ratings For submenu.

11. On the last four items, choose the highest level of rating that a piece of content can have for it to be used. For instance, under Movies you can choose to allow only PG-13 or lower. You can also choose Allow All Movies or Don't Allow Movies.

12. Use Allowed Content to determine whether In-App Purchases of paid app content, such as game levels or magazine issues, are allowed.

13. After an in-app purchase is made, the password won't be required for future in-app purchases for 15 minutes. But you can change that here to require it again immediately.

14. Select options in the Game Center functions you want to allow. This will only affect games that use Game Center to communicate with other players. Some apps use their own system of communication or other systems like Facebook.

15. When a new app is installed, it can ask for permission to access and change your contacts, events, reminders, and photos. With these settings you can prevent new apps from gaining this permission. You also get to see a list of which apps have this permission and can deny it.

16. You can shut off app access to your Twitter and Facebook accounts. Note that this relates to Twitter and Facebook accounts added to your iPad through the Settings app—for example, the ability to use the Photos app to post a photo to your Facebook account. If you have an app that doesn't go through your iPad's settings, such as the official Facebook app, you need to sign out of Facebook inside that app to prevent someone from using it.

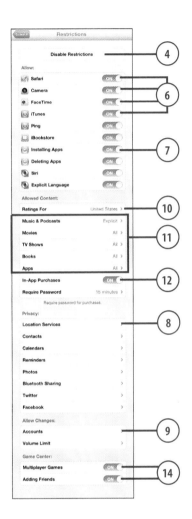

Privacy Settings

The permission settings in step 15 are also available outside of parental controls. You can select Privacy on the left side of the Settings app and then view all the apps that have requested access to contacts, events, reminders, photos, and your location. You can review and deny access to these apps.

It's Not All Good

SETTINGS NOT REMEMBERED

It would be nice if you could just switch Restrictions on and off, so you could hand off your iPad to Junior after quickly turning them on, but the settings are reset each time. So you need to set the switches each time after turning Restrictions back on.

Setting Side Switch Functionality

When the original iPad came out, the side switch was an orientation lock. It was very useful for fixing the orientation while reading a book. But then Apple changed the functionality of the switch with a software update and turned it into a mute switch like the iPhone has. That made a lot of people unhappy. So starting with iOS 4.3 and after, you get to choose what you want the side button to do.

1. Tap the Settings icon on the Home screen.

2. Tap General.

3. Choose Lock Rotation if you want your side switch to be an orientation lock switch.

4. Choose Mute if you want the side switch to mute the volume on the speakers and earphones.

Setting Your Date and Time

You can set the date, time and time zone for your iPad and even choose whether to display the time in 12- or 24-hour mode.

1. Tap the Settings icon on the Home screen.

2. Tap General.

3. Scroll down to the bottom of the General Settings list and tap Date & Time.

4. Set the 24-Hour Time switch to your preference.

5. Turning Set Automatically on will sync the date and time with the Wi-Fi network or wireless network that the iPad is connected to.

6. Tap the Time Zone button and then enter the name of your city, or a nearby city, to set the zone.

7. Tap the Set Date & Time to bring up date and time controls.

8. Tap either the day or the time at the top of the control to switch the bottom of the control to the correct interface. If you choose the time, you can set the hour and minute. If you choose the date, you can set the month, day, and year.

Modifying Keyboard Settings

If you use your iPad for email or word processing, you will use the on-screen keyboard a lot. The keyboard does several things to make it easier for you to type, but some of these might get in the way of your typing style. Use the following steps to modify the keyboard settings to your preferences.

1. Tap the Settings icon on the Home screen.

2. Tap General.

3. Scroll down to the bottom of the General Settings list and tap Keyboard.

4. Turn Auto-Capitalization on to automatically make the first character of a name or a sentence a capital letter.

5. Turn Auto-Correction on to have mistyped words automatically corrected.

6. Turn Check Spelling on or off to control whether possible misspellings are indicated.

7. Turn Enable Caps Lock on or off. By default, this is off. When Caps Lock is enabled, you double-tap the shift key to lock it.

8. Turn on the "." Shortcut if you want a double-tap of the spacebar to insert a period followed by a space.

9. Use the Keyboards button to choose a different keyboard layout. In addition to keyboards commonly used in other countries, you can switch to a Dvorak keyboard or one of several other alternatives to the traditional QWERTY keyboard.

10. If you want to lock the keyboard so it can never be split and moved up vertically, then switch this to off. See "Using the On-Screen Keyboard" in Chapter 1.

11. You can add your own shortcuts. For instance, when you type "omw," it will instantly expand to "On my way!" Add your own shortcuts for things you commonly type.

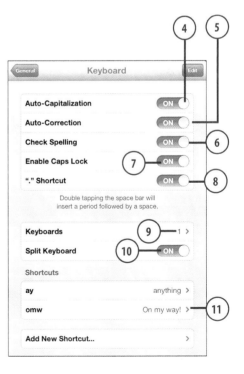

Changing Safari Settings

We look at the Safari web browser in Chapter 7, "Surfing the Web," but you can customize it right here in the Settings app.

1. Tap the Settings icon on the Home screen.

2. Tap Safari from the list of settings on the left.

3. Select which search engine to use. Google is the default, but you can also choose Yahoo! or Bing.

4. Adjust your AutoFill settings for filling out forms on the web. Your iPad can pull from your contact info in the Contacts app or from data you previously filled in on the same or similar web pages. Set Names and Passwords to On to have Safari remember your username and passwords for some websites.

5. Decide whether you want to immediately jump to a new tab, or stay on the current page when you open a new tab and let the tab open silently in the background.

6. Choose whether to show the Bookmarks bar all the time or only when you have saved bookmarks in the bookmarks bar.

7. Fraud Warning checks websites against a public database of websites to avoid. I recommend leaving this switch on. If you try to follow a link to one of these sites, you get a warning and a chance to change your mind before loading the page.

Changing Music Settings

You have a few preferences to choose from when it comes to music playback. Most of them have to do with the quality and volume of sound you get from your iPad.

1. Tap the Settings icon on the Home screen.

2. Choose Music from the list of settings on the left.

3. Turn Sound Check on or off to play your music at approximately the same volume level, even if the song files themselves are louder or softer than each other.

4. Use EQ to select an equalizer setting. You can select from an equalizer setting according to the type of music you listen to, or settings like "Spoken Word," "Small Speakers," or "Bass Booster."

5. Tap Volume Limit to set a limit on the maximum volume.

6. Tap to turn on iTunes Match. iTunes Match is a service where all the music you own is stored on Apple's servers, and you can access it with iTunes on a Mac or PC and through the Music app on your iPad, iPhone, or iPod Touch. See www.apple.com/itunes/itunes-match/ for more information.

7. Enter your Apple ID and password information to allow streaming music and video from your Mac. See "Home Sharing" in Chapter 4.

Notification Center Settings

From time to time, apps will need to interrupt what you are doing or alert you even when you are not using your iPad. In iOS 6, this is unified through the Notifications Center. The Notifications Center will give you alerts in one of two ways: as a box in the middle of your screen or as a drop-down notification from the top. You can change this setting for each app in the Notifications section of the Settings app.

Note that the specific options will vary for each app. For instance, Messages has settings for showing a preview of the message and for repeating the notification, but Calendar doesn't have those options.

1. Tap the Notifications category in Settings.

2. Do Not Disturb mode silences almost all notifications. You can set a specific time period, such as 10:00 PM to 7:00 AM for Do Not Disturb mode. You can also allow FaceTime calls from people in a specific contacts group to ring regardless of the current setting. Another option with Do Not Disturb is to allow a second call within three minutes from the same person to ring.

3. You can also turn on Do Not Disturb mode with this switch on the left side of your Settings app.

4. Tap any app to view its notifications settings. If an app isn't listed, it doesn't send out any notifications.

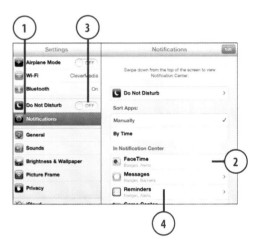

5. You can remove an app from the Notifications Center so it doesn't send any notifications.

6. You can limit the number of items that the Notifications Center shows for this particular app at one time.

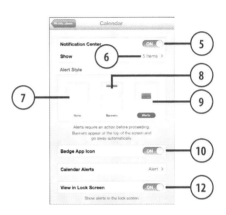

7. Choosing the None alert style means that neither a banner nor alert will appear.

8. Choosing Banners means that a drop-down banner will appear when the app has a message, and it will go away on its own after a few seconds. These do not interrupt your work when they appear.

9. Choosing Alerts means that a box pops up in the middle of the screen when the app has a message, and you must dismiss it to continue.

10. Badge App Icon means that the icon will show a number over it when there is a message.

11. Many apps let you set the specific sound used.

12. View in Lock Screen means that alerts from this app will appear even when the iPad is locked.

More Settings

Too many settings categories exist to cover all of them here, but the following are a few other key items.

1. Tap Videos.

2. Adjust whether a video starts playing where you left off or at the beginning each time.

3. Turn Closed Captioning on or off.

4. Tap Maps.

5. Decide whether you would like to see distances displayed in miles or kilometers.

6. Decide whether labels should be in English, regardless of the region of the map displayed.

7. Choose a size for map labels.

Adding More and More Apps

The Settings app adds new pages as you add new apps to your iPad. Some third-party apps do not add a component in the Settings app, so don't be alarmed if you don't see an app you added in the Settings list.

Sync your music and
information with your Mac
or PC computer.

Put your favorite
photos on your iPad.

In this chapter, you find out how to connect your iPad to your local Wi-Fi network. You also see how to sync your iPad with your Mac or Windows computer.

Networking and Syncing

Now that you have a new iPad, why not introduce it to your old friend—your computer? They have a lot in common. And they are both good at sharing—particularly information such as your contacts, calendar, music, video, and documents.

Syncing your iPad to your Mac or PC is something you want to do right away and continue to do on a regular basis. This way you get all your data from your computer onto your iPad, and as you add new information and media to either device, they can share it so it is always at your fingertips.

Setting Up Your Wi-Fi Network Connection

One of the first things you need to do with your iPad, even before you sync it to your computer, is to establish an Internet connection.

Chances are that you did this when you started your iPad for the first time. It should have prompted you to choose from a list of nearby Wi-Fi networks. But you do this again if you first used your iPad away from home or need to switch to use another Wi-Fi network.

To connect your iPad to a wireless network, follow these steps.

1. Tap the Settings icon on the Home screen.

2. Choose Wi-Fi from the list of settings on the left.

3. Make sure that Wi-Fi is turned on.

4. Tap the item that represents your network. (If you tap on the blue-circled right arrow next to each network, you can further customize your network settings.)

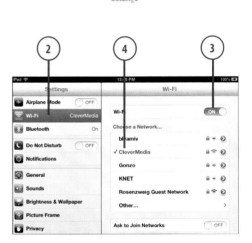

I Don't Have a Wireless Network

If you don't have a Wi-Fi network but do have high-speed Internet through a telephone or cable provider, you have several options. The first is to call your provider and ask for a new network modem that enables wireless connections. Some providers might upgrade your box for free or a small cost.

Another option is to keep your current box and add a wireless base station of your own, such as the Apple Airport Extreme base station.

5. If the network is protected by a password, you will be asked to enter the password. Once you enter the password, your iPad will remember it. So if you switch between two locations, like work and home, you will be asked to enter the password for each the first time you use that connection. From that point on, your iPad will automatically log on to each connection as you move around.

SECURITY? YES!

Your wireless network at home should have security turned on. This means that you should see a padlock next to it in the list of Wi-Fi networks on your iPad. When you select it for the first time, you should be asked to supply a password.

If you don't require a password, seriously consider changing your Wi-Fi network box's settings to add security. The issue isn't simply about requiring a password to use your Internet connection. It is about the fact that a secure network will send encrypted data through the air. Otherwise, anyone can simply "sniff" your wireless connection and see what you are doing online—such as using credit cards and logging on to membership sites. See your network equipment's documentation to set up security.

Setting Up Your 3G/4G Connection

If you have an iPad with 3G/4G capabilities, you can set it up to use AT&T, Verizon, or any other compatible network. You can purchase a monthly data plan or purchase service in shorter increments.

1. Tap the Settings icon on the Home screen.

2. Tap Cellular Data on the left.

3. Turn on Cellular Data. In addition, if you have a 3rd generation iPad mini, turn on Enable LTE for the faster 4G connection.

4. Tap View Account.

5. Next, you are prompted to create an account with a service. The service will be either AT&T or Verizon in the U.S., depending on which iPad model you own. You'll need to enter all your basic information and specify an email address for your account and a password.

6. Choose a data plan.

7. Enter your credit card information. When you are done, you have to approve the service agreement and confirm your purchase. Still, it beats going to the mall and dealing with a salesperson at a mobile phone store, right?

8. Tap OK. It may take a few more minutes for your 4G service to activate.

9. After establishing 4G service you can view your usage and renew your plan at any time by following steps 1, 2, and 4 again. Then you can see your play details and status. Tap Add Data or Change Plan to renew or increase your data plan.

---

⑦   **⑥**

Cellular Data Account   Cancel

Recurring Domestic Plan Options

The selected plan will start immediately. Your credit card will automatically be billed every 30 days, on the date your current plan ends.

Use the www.att.com/datacalculator to determine which plan is right for you.

250 MB of data for 30 days - LTE for $14.99	✓
3GB of data for 30 days - LTE for $30.00	
5GB of data for 30 days - LTE for $50.00	

Payment & Billing Information

Visa ✓   MasterCard   Discover   Amex

credit card   Number

name   as it appears on the card

expiration date   MM   YYYY

security code   3 or 4 digits printed on front or back of card

---

SIM PIN

Data Plan Activated

Your AT&T cellular data plan has been successfully activated.

⑧   **OK**

Cellular Data Account   Cancel

Rethink Possible 📶

Account Overview
Cellular Data Number: 303-333-3333

data plan   **3GB of data for 30 days - LTE of domestic dat...**

status   **1 MB used / 3071 MB left for 29 days**

billing period   **03/17/12 to 04/16/12**   **⑨**

Add Data or Change Plan   >

Add International Plan   >

Edit User & Payment Information   >

View Full Account Overview...

OK

Working with Wi-Fi and 3G/4G

After you establish a 3G/4G plan, your iPad should still connect to your Wi-Fi networks when it is in range and use 3G when it cannot find a Wi-Fi network. You can also return to Settings and turn on or off Cellular Data to specifically prevent your iPad from using the 3G network. This is handy when you are completely out of mobile data range but have local Wi-Fi; for instance, you might be on an airplane flight. Of course, for take-off and landing, you will most likely be asked to use the Airplane Mode available in the Settings as well. That mode comes in handy when you want to quickly take your iPad "off the grid" and have it connected to absolutely nothing.

Looking at the top-left corner of your iPad's screen, you can tell which sort of connection you are currently using. The first image shows an iPad with no 3G/4G connection at all, only Wi-Fi. The second shows an iPad with a 3G/4G connection, but currently a Wi-Fi connection is being used for data. In this case, all data is coming from Wi-Fi and you are not using your mobile data bandwidth at all. The third image shows an iPad that is using the 3G/4G connection for data at the moment.

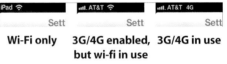

| Wi-Fi only | 3G/4G enabled, but wi-fi in use | 3G/4G in use |

It's Not All Good

WATCH FOR DATA ROAMING

In the Cellular Data settings, you can turn Data Roaming on or off. This is what enables your iPad to connect to wireless data networks that are outside of your data plan, such as networks in other countries. If you leave Data Roaming on and your iPad connects to such a network, you may find a surprise bill in the mail. You can avoid extra charges by leaving Data Roaming off or by purchasing a plan from AT&T for International data roaming.

Syncing with iTunes

Whether you are on a Mac or PC, you need iTunes to sync your iPad with your computer. If you are on a Mac, you already have iTunes. All you need to do is run Software Update to make sure you have the latest version. If you run Windows, you can get the Windows version of iTunes from Apple's site: http://www.apple.com/itunes/download/.

There are many advantages to syncing your iPad with a computer.

- Each day you sync your iPad, iTunes stores a backup of its content. You can restore all your data from these backups if you lose your iPad.

- Syncing with a computer is the only way to get a large number of photos from your collection on your iPad.

- Syncing is how you get your music stored in iTunes onto your iPad. If you have a large collection of music, you can opt to copy only a selection of it to your iPad at any one time.

- It can be easier to arrange your app icons on the Home screen pages using iTunes, rather than doing it on your iPad.

- On a Mac in the Calendar app, you have far greater control over setting recurring and special events, which appear on your iPad in the Calendar app, even though you cannot create them there.

You might get a message on your computer the first time you connect your iPad and open iTunes, asking if it is okay to sync your iPad to this computer. The message won't reappear.

After connecting the first time, iTunes should automatically open when you connect your iPad. While connected, you can always resync to apply changes by clicking the Sync button in iTunes.

You can also check Sync over Wi-Fi connection in your iPad's options in iTunes. This allows you to sync when your iPad isn't connected by the cable. It only needs to be on the same network as your Mac or PC that is running iTunes.

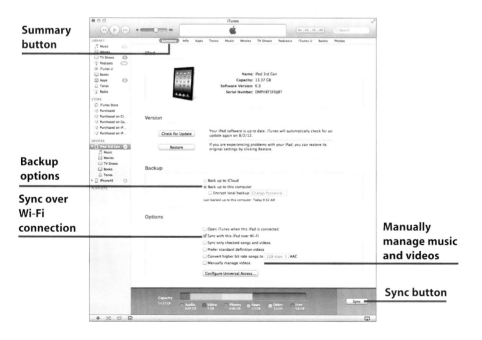

Summary
button

Backup
options

Sync over
Wi-Fi
connection

Manually
manage music
and videos

Sync button

After your device is in sync, you can change some general options for your iPad from the Summary screen in iTunes. Most of the options are self-explanatory, such as Open iTunes When this iPad Is Connected.

One option that dramatically changes how your iPad syncs is Manually Manage Music and Videos, which turns off automatic syncing of music and videos and enables you to simply drag and drop songs and movies from your iTunes library onto the iPad icon on the left. (You might need to scroll down the Summary page to locate this checkbox if your screen size is too small to show the entire page at once.)

As we look at some of the syncing options for the iPad, the Mac version of iTunes is used as an example. The Windows version of iTunes is similar but not exactly the same. One difference is that on a Mac, iTunes syncs data with Mac applications such as Address Book, iCal, and iPhoto. On Windows, iTunes must find this data elsewhere.

BACK IT UP!

Perhaps the most important part of syncing with your computer is backing up your data. Everything you create with apps, every preference you carefully set, and every photo you take could be gone in a second if you drop your iPad or someone swipes it. Even a hardware failure is possible—the iPad isn't perfect.

Choosing Back up to this computer is your best option. This saves all your data on your computer in a backup file. Try to do it once per day. With a good backup you can replace a lost iPad and restore all your data from the backup. It works incredibly well.

You can always plug your iPad into your Mac or PC, launch iTunes, and Control+click (right-click on Windows) your iPad in the left sidebar and select Backup. But it also happens automatically once per day if you sync.

Your other option is Back up to iCloud. This will back up your data wirelessly to iCloud. It is your only option if you are not going to sync your iPad with a computer. But it does use up your data storage allotment in your iCloud account, so you may need to upgrade your iCloud account to allow for more data.

Even so, Back up to iCloud is a great alternative, especially if you travel often and use your iPad for critical tasks.

Syncing Contacts, Calendars, and Other Information

Use the Info page in iTunes to sync your contacts, calendars, and a few other things to your iPad.

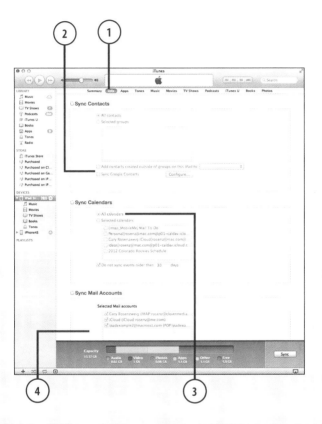

1. Click the Info button in iTunes to see options for choosing how to sync your contacts. You can sync all your contacts from Address Book or sync only selected groups.

2. You can also sync with contacts you have stored with either Yahoo! or Google. You need to enter your login information so that iTunes can access the contacts on that service.

3. Choose to sync all the calendars in iCal or just selected ones. In addition, you can choose not to sync old events.

4. Next, you can sync email accounts with Apple's Mail program, which syncs the settings between your computer and your iPad, not the mail messages. See Chapter 8, "Communicating with Email, Messaging, and Twitter," for more on getting mail on your iPad.

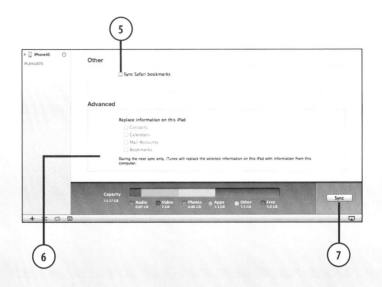

5. To transfer your Mac's bookmarks to your iPad and keep the bookmarks synced between the iPad and the Mac, check the Sync Safari Bookmarks check box.

6. Use the Advanced options (Contacts, Calendars, Mail Accounts, and Bookmarks) to indicate that during the next sync the information should be erased from your iPad and replaced with the corresponding information from your Mac or PC.

7. Click the Sync button to sync.

It's Not All Good

DUPLICATE CALENDARS

If you are already using iCloud to sync your calendar, don't also add it using iTunes. Doing so may give you two copies of all those events: one copy synced over the Internet, and one synced each time you connect to iTunes. Just use iCloud syncing and leave Sync iCal Calendars unchecked. Same for contacts.

Syncing Apps

iTunes keeps your apps on your computer and your iPad in sync and helps you organize them.

Note that you cannot run apps on your computer, just store them. You can store all of the apps you have downloaded and purchased on your computer and only have a subset of those set to sync on to your iPad.

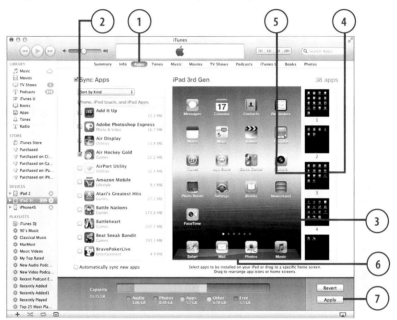

1. Click the Apps button of your iPad's settings in iTunes.

2. Use the list on the left to check or uncheck apps to determine which ones to sync with your iPad.

3. Drag the app icons around on the representation of the Home screen page.

Go Ahead—Select More Than One

You can click more than one app icon in iTunes and then drag them around as groups. This makes it easy to rearrange your apps in iTunes and is the reason many people do it here, rather than on the iPad itself.

4. Select another Home screen page by clicking a page on the right.

5. You can drag an app from the main representation to another page on the right to move it to another page.

6. You can also drag apps in and out of the iPad's dock area at the bottom.

7. Click the Apply button if you want to apply the changes now.

Syncing Documents

Apps sometimes have documents. For example, Pages is a word processor, so it would naturally have word-processing documents. Documents are stored on your iPad, but you might want to access them on your Mac or PC as well.

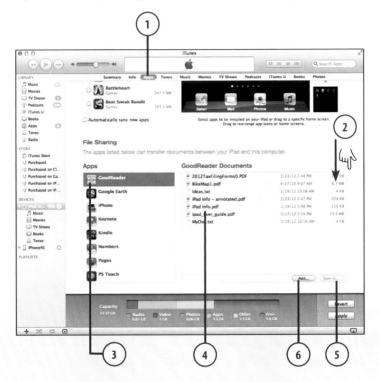

1.   Click the Apps button of your iPad's settings in iTunes.

2.   Scroll down to the bottom of the Apps page.

3.   In the File Sharing section, choose an app.

No File Sharing Section?

The File Sharing section on the Apps screen will only appear if you have at least one app that is capable of sharing files through iTunes. Examples would be Pages, Numbers, Keynote, iMovie, GarageBand, Voice Memos, and GoodReader.

4. Select a document from the right.

5. Click the Save To button to save the document as a file on your computer.

6. Click the Add button to import a file from your computer to your iPad. Each app has its own document space on your iPad. So if you have two PDF readers, and you want the PDF document available to both, you need to add it to each app's documents.

Drag and Drop

You can also use drag and drop to pull documents out of, and import them into, the app's document space.

Sync with iCloud

If you are using iCloud and the app supports it, then documents can sync automatically and wirelessly. For instance, if you are using Pages on your Mac with OS X Mountain Lion, and you save a Pages document to iCloud, you will see that document appear in your list of Pages documents on your iPad as well. Both your Mac and your iPad must be using the same iCloud account to enable you to work on the same document, while switching between your Mac and your iPad, with no need to sync in between.

Other apps may not support iCloud, so using iTunes to sync may be your only choice to move documents back and forth. See the section, "Syncing Using iCloud," later in this chapter to set up iCloud.

Syncing Music

The easy way to sync music is to select Entire Music Library In iTunes on your computer. If you have more music than can fit on your iPad, though, you must make some choices. Syncing Movies, TV Shows, Podcasts, Tones (ringtones for messaging and FaceTime), iTunes U, and Books all work in a similar way to syncing music, so you can apply what you learn in these steps to those items as well.

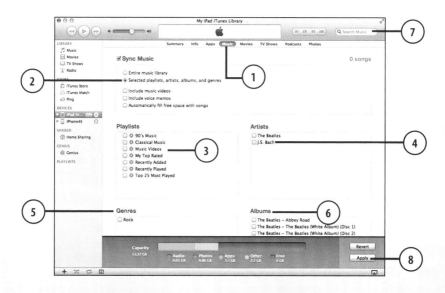

1. Click the Music button of your iPad's settings in iTunes.

2. Click the Selected Playlists, Artists, and Genres button.

3. Check off any playlists in the Playlists section that you want to include.

4. Check off any artists for which you want to include every song by that artist.

5. Check off any genres to include in their entirety.

6. Check off any albums you want to include.

7. Use the search box to quickly find specific artists.

8. Click the Apply button if you want to apply the changes now.

One Copy Only

Note that songs are never duplicated on your iPad. So for instance, if the same song appears in two playlists and is also by an artist that you have selected to sync, the song only has one copy on your iPad. But it appears in both of the playlists and under that artist, album, and alphabetical list of all songs.

CHECK IT OFF

Another way to select songs to sync with your iPad is to use the Entire Music Library option but also choose Sync Only Checked Songs and Videos from the Summary tab. Then you can pick and choose each song that syncs.

Another option is to strictly use playlists to sync without checking off any artists or genres. Then, in addition to your normal playlists, create one called For iPad and put every song in there that you want on your iPad. Then set that playlist to sync.

Or Use iTunes Match

iTunes Match is a service from Apple. For an annual fee, you can sync your music collection with Apple's servers. Then you can access all your music on your iPad by turning iTunes Match on in the Music settings in the Settings app. When you do this, you no longer need to sync your music. Instead, you see all your music on your iPad, and it will download from Apple's servers when you want to listen to a particular song.

Visit http://www.apple.com/itunes/itunes-match/ to find out more about Apple's iTunes Match service.

The Kitchen Sync

In addition to Music, you can also sync your Tones, Movies, TV Shows, Podcasts, iTunes U, and Books in a similar way. Each type of media has its own way of syncing, but they are all similar to music. For instance, Tones lets you sync all tones or selected tones, and then you select them individually. There are no playlists for Tones. Movies, TV Shows, and Podcasts can be included in playlists, so syncing options there let you sync by playlist if you like. Explore each page of your syncing settings to see which options you have.

Syncing Photos

Syncing your photos actually isn't that much different than syncing music. You can choose to have all your photos transferred to your iPad, or choose them by albums, events, or faces.

1. Click the Photos button of your iPad's settings in iTunes.

2. Click the Sync Photos From check box. If you use iPhoto, you should choose iPhoto from the drop-down menu. Other choices for Mac users include choosing any folder or the Pictures folder.

   If you use Windows, you can choose your My Pictures folder or another folder. Any subfolders are treated as albums, and you can select or deselect any of them.

   You might sync photos to your iPad by selecting a photo tool, such as Photoshop Elements, as your sync companion. If you choose that program, you can use the groupings in that program as albums.

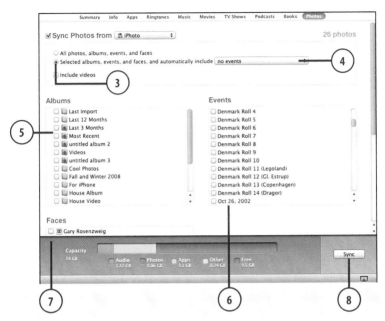

3. Choose whether to sync all photos or only selected ones.

4. If you choose selected photos, you can also choose a number of recent events or all events from a recent period of time.

5. Select any albums that you want to sync.

6. Select specific events you want to sync.

7. You can also select to sync all photos tagged for a specific person in iPhoto.

8. Click the Sync button to apply the changes.

No Duplicates

Like with music, you get only one copy of each photo, no matter how many times the photo appears in albums, events, and faces. The photos appear in all the right places but take up only one spot in memory on your iPad.

It's Not All Good

ONE WAY ONLY

Like with the iPhone and iPod touch, syncing photo albums works only one way. For the photos you sync from your computer to your iPad, you cannot pull photos from your iPad back to your computer. Syncing photos from your computer to your iPad works only one way. The original is on your computer, and there is merely a smaller copy on your iPad. So, it is important that you maintain your real photo library on your computer and remember to back it up.

Syncing Using iCloud

If you have an iCloud account from Apple, you can sync parts of your iPad's data wirelessly even if you are not in the same location. If you do not yet have an iCloud account, it is easy to sign up for a free one. You may have already set one up while going through the initial welcome screens when you first turned on your iPad.

1. Tap the Settings icon on the Home screen and then tap iCloud.

2. If you already have an iCloud account, enter your Apple ID and password and then tap the Sign In button.

3. Tap the Get a Free Apple ID button to create a new Apple ID if you have never used one before. If you already have an account with iTunes, iBooks, the iOS App Store, or the Mac App Store, then you already have an Apple ID and should use that in step 2.

4. Choose which pieces of data you want to sync with your iCloud account.

5. You can turn on iCloud mail to use an @icloud.com email account. The first time you turn this on, you will be asked to create a new @icloud.com email address. Even if you don't plan on switching to that new address for your personal correspondence, it doesn't hurt to create this email address now, as it is free.

6. Enable Photo Stream to use iCloud's Photo Stream feature. See the sidebar "What Is Photo Stream?" in Chapter 9.

7. Turn on Documents & Data to allow some apps to store documents on the iCloud servers instead of your local iPad's memory. This makes that data available to your other iOS devices as well. Not all apps have this functionality, however.

8. Enabling Find My iPad lets you use this feature to locate your iPad if you have lost it or it has been stolen.

Creating a New Apple ID

If you choose, in step 3, to create a new Apple ID because you have never had an account before, the process is pretty simple. You'll be asked for information in a short series of screens: your birthday, name, email address, and a security question. The email address you give will become your Apple ID, so it must be an email address that you already use. You'll be given the chance to create a new @icloud.com email address later on. A verification email will be sent to the email address you provide, and you must open that email and click a link in it to activate your account before you proceed.

No Email Please

If you do not use your iCloud email account, you can just switch off Mail in your iCloud settings. You can still sync the other data and use Find My iPad. Many people choose to use iCloud for features like bookmark and calendar syncing and don't use their @ icloud.com email addresses for anything.

Keeping Your iPad Up-to-Date

Apple periodically comes out with updates to iOS. And Apple and other developers come out with updates to apps all the time. Usually all these updates are free and contain useful and important new features. So, there is no reason not to keep your iPad up-to-date. In fact, updates sometimes include important security patches, so you should pay careful attention when an update is available.

1. Tap the Settings icon on the Home screen and then tap General.

2. Tap Software Update.

3. If you have the latest version of iOS, you will see a message like this one. Otherwise, follow the instructions provided to update your iPad.

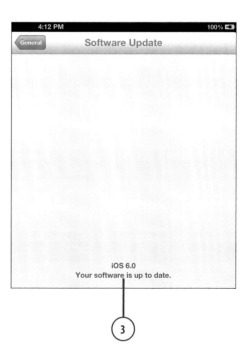

4. On the Home screen, find and tap the App Store app. You may also notice a number in a red circle attached to the icon. This tells you how many apps you have that have updates available.

5. Tap the Updates button. This takes you to a screen with a list of all available app updates.

6. Tap any app's Free button to immediately download the updated version of that app.

7. Tap Update All instead to download and install all updates.

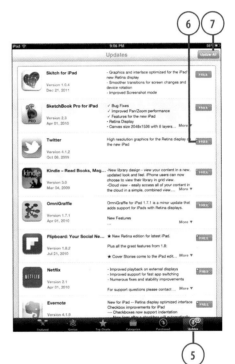

Purchase music and
buy or rent videos.

Listen to Podcasts

Play your music.

In this chapter, you learn how to use the
Music and Video apps to play music and
watch video.

→ Playing a Song
→ Building a Playlist
→ Making iTunes Purchases
→ Downloading Podcasts
→ Playing Video
→ Using AirPlay to Play Music and Video
  on Other Devices
→ Home Sharing

Playing Music and Video

The iPad handles playing music as well as any iPod or iPhone
ever has, plus it has a big screen for you to use to browse your
collection.

Playing a Song

So let's start by simply selecting and playing a song with the Music app.

1. Tap the Music icon, which is most likely along the bottom of your Home screen.

2. Tap Songs on the bottom if it isn't already selected.

3. Tap the name of a song to start it.

Playing iTunes Match Music

If you are using iTunes Match, you will see all your music in the list, even songs not currently on your iPad. You can still tap the name of a song to start it. The song will download and play, assuming you are connected to the Internet. You can also tap the iTunes Match (cloud) icon for each song to simply download each song so it is ready to listen to later, even if you are not connected. You would want to do this for some songs if you are going to be away from your Internet connection and plan to listen to music.

Visit http://www.apple.com/itunes/ itunes-match/ to find out more about Apple's iTunes Match service.

4. At the top of the screen, the square Play button changes to a Pause button. The red time prog-ress bar to the right begins to move.

5. Use the volume slider at the top to adjust the volume, or use the physical volume controls.

6. Tap the album art at the top to enlarge it.

7. With the artwork on the screen, tap in the middle to bring back up the play and volume controls, along with the name of the artist, song, and album.

8. Tap the repeat button to make your iPad repeat all songs in the list. Tap the Repeat button a second time to repeat the current song over and over.

9. Tap the Shuffle button to make your iPad play the songs in the list in a random order.

10. Tap the left-facing arrow button at the bottom left to return to the main Music app interface.

How Else Can I Listen to Music?

You can also listen to music using other third-party apps. Some apps access your music collection on your iPad, but the most interesting ones play streaming music from over the Internet. We look at apps, such as Pandora, in Chapter 15.

11. Tap any of the buttons at the bottom of the screen—Playlists, Songs, Artists, and Albums —to sort the list of songs.

12. When you sort by albums or genres, you will see a grid of album covers. Just tap on any album to view the album and the songs in it. Tap a song name to play it.

13. Tap in the Search field in the lower right to search your song list.

Siri: Playing Music

You can use Siri to play music. Here are some examples:

"Play The Beatles"

"Play Georgia On My Mind"

"Play some blues"

"Play my driving music" (plays the playlist named "driving music")

"Shuffle all songs"

"Skip"

"Pause"

CONTROLLING MUSIC PLAYBACK

To control music playback

- Tap and move the red line in the progress bar at the top of the screen to move around inside a song.

- Use the Back and Forward buttons at the top of the screen to move from song to song in the list of currently selected songs.

- Press the Pause button at any time to pause the music. Use the same button, which has become a Play button, to restart the music.

Building a Playlist

You can create playlists on your Mac or PC in iTunes, but you can also build actual playlists on your iPad.

1. Tap the Playlists button in the bottom-left corner of the main Music app screen.

2. A list of current playlists appears. Tap the New button.

3. Give the new playlist a name and tap Save.

4. In the expanded list of your music, tap the + buttons next to each song you want to add to the play-list.

5. Tap the Sort buttons at the bot-tom of the screen to sort through your music.

6. Use the Search field in the lower right to find songs faster.

7. Tap the Done button when you have selected all the songs you want to add to the playlist.

Genius Playlists

If you turn on the Genius feature in your Mac or PC copy of iTunes, you can use the Genius playlist feature to create playlists. After you click the Atom icon, select a song to use as the start of the Genius playlist. iTunes selects other songs from your collection that are similar and creates a play-list using the name of that song.

8. On the playlist edit screen, remove songs from the playlist by tapping on the red buttons.

9. Tap and drag on the three-line buttons to rearrange the songs.

10. Tap Done to complete the playlist. The next time you sync your iPad to iTunes, the new playlist syncs, too.

Add songs to the "My Playlist" playlist

A		
Ain't Nobody's Bizness (Live At Sa...	B.B. King	Live At San Quentin
Ain't That Fine	Ray Charles	The Essential Collection
Alfie	Lily Allen	Alright, Still
All Down The Line	The Rolling Stones	Exile On Main Street
Analogous	I Am The World Trade Center	Out of the Loop
Animal Boy	Ramones	Mania
Asking For It	Hole	Live Through This
Atomic	Blondie	The Best Of Blondie
Aurora Borealis	I Am The World Trade Center	Out of the Loop
B		
Baby Won't You Please Come Home	Ray Charles	The Essential Collection
Bad Moon Rising	Creedence Clearwater Revi...	Chronicle, Volume I
Ball And Chain	Social Distortion	Social Distortion
B.B.King Intro (Live At San Quentin)	B.B. King	Live At San Quentin
Beat On The Brat	Ramones	Mania
Beyond The Sea	Bobby Darin	The Hit Singles Collection
Blank Expression	Lily Allen	Alright, Still
Blitzkrieg Bop	Ramones	Mania
Blueberry Hill	Louis Armstrong	All-Time Greatest Hits
Bonzo Goes To Bitburg	Ramones	Mania
Boplicity	Miles Davis	Birth Of The Cool
Boo 'Til You Drop	Ramones	Mania

Songs | Artists | Albums | Genres | More

My Playlist

⊖	1.	Ain't That Fine	Ray Charles	The Essential Collection
⊖	2.	Hey Tonight	Creedence Clearwater Revi...	Chronicle, Volume I
⊖	3.	It's Sweet	Liz Phair	Liz Phair
⊖	4.	Lookin' Out My Back Door	Creedence Clearwater Revi...	Chronicle, Volume I
⊖	5.	Only Love Can Break Your Heart	Juliana Hatfield	Gold Stars 1992 - 2002 : The...
⊖	6.	Ring Of Fire	Social Distortion	Social Distortion
⊖	7.	Soul Survivor	The Rolling Stones	Exile On Main Street
⊖	8.	Thrill Is Gone (Live At San Que...	B.B. King	Live At San Quentin

Making iTunes Purchases

You have lots of options when it comes to adding more music to your iPad. You can simply add more music to your iTunes collection on your computer and then sync those songs to your iPad. In that case, you can buy them from iTunes, from another online source, or import them from music CDs.

How Else Can I Get Music?

You can purchase music on your iPad only through the iTunes app. But you can sync music from your computer that you get from any source that doesn't use special copy protection, like CDs you import into iTunes. You can buy online from places such as Amazon.com, eMusic.com, cdbaby.com, or even directly from the websites of some artists.

In addition to syncing music to your iPad from your computer, you can purchase music, movies, TV shows, and audio books directly on your iPad using the iTunes app and using the same account that you use in iTunes on your computer.

1. Tap the iTunes app icon on your Home screen to go to the iTunes store.

2. Use the buttons at the top of the screen to choose which genre of music to view.

3. Swipe the section lists left and right to browse more featured albums.

4. Use the Search field at the top to search for an artist, album, or song by name.

5. Drag the screen up to reveal more lists, such as top albums, top songs, and music videos.

6. Select a suggestion from the list, or tap the Search button on the keyboard to complete the search.

7. Find an album you want to buy, and tap its artwork to view more information.

Syncing Devices

After you make an iTunes purchase, the music, TV show, or movie you downloaded should transfer to your computer the next time you sync your iPad. From your computer, you can sync your new purchase to any other device you use that uses your iTunes account.

8. Tap a song name to listen to a sample of the song.

9. Tap outside of the album window to close it and return to the previous view.

10. To buy a song, album, or any item in the iTunes music store, tap the price of that item and then tap again on the Buy button.

How About My Home Videos?

If you shoot a home video with a video camera, or iPod touch or iPhone, you can bring that into iTunes on your Mac or PC and sync it to your iPad. They appear as Movies, right next to your purchased content.

What About My DVDs?

If you can import CD music content into iTunes, you'd think you'd be able to import video content from your DVDs. Well, technically it is possible (although not necessarily legal) by using programs like Handbrake (http://handbrake.fr/) for your Mac or PC to import DVD content and then drag the resulting file into iTunes. Then you can sync it with your iPad.

BUYING AND RENTING VIDEO

Although the process of buying video is essentially the same as buying music, some significant details are different. It is worth taking a look at these details so that you know what you are getting into before spending your money.

Copy Protection   Although music in the iTunes store recently became copy-protection free, videos are a different story altogether. Purchased videos can be played back only on the Apple devices you own that use your iTunes account. You can't burn videos to a DVD, for instance, or watch them on a TV unless it is hooked up to an Apple device. Rentals are even more strict because you can watch them only on the device you rent them on.

Collecting Movies   Thinking of starting a collection of videos by purchasing them from Apple? These videos take up a lot of space on your hard drive. An iPad, even a 64GB version, quickly fills up if you start adding dozens of movies.

Time-Delayed Rentals   Rentals have some strict playback restrictions. After you download a rental, you have 30 days to watch it. After you start watching it, you have only 24 hours to finish it. This means you can load up your iPad in advance with a few movies to watch on an airplane flight or while on vacation.

TV Show Season Passes   You can purchase seasons of TV shows that aren't complete yet. When you do this, you are basically pre-ordering each episode. You get the existing episodes immediately but have to wait for the future episodes. They usually appear the next day after airing on network television.

Multi-Pass   In addition to season passes, you can also get a Multi-Pass, which is for TV shows that broadcast daily. When you purchase a Multi-Pass, you get the most recent episode plus the next 15 episodes when they become available.

HD Versus SD   You can purchase or rent most movies and TV shows in either HD (high definition) or SD (standard definition). The difference is the quality of the image, which affects the file size, of course. If you have a slow connection or limited bandwidth, you might want to stick to SD versions of the shows.

iCloud Movies   If you use iCloud, some movies that you purchase (not rent) will appear in your Videos app as well, even if they are not actually on your iPad. You will see a little iCloud icon appear next to them. You can tap that icon to start downloading that movie to your iPad from Apple's servers. This allows you to purchase movies from Apple and not have to worry about where to store them. Simply download them from Apple any time you want to watch. But this only works if the movie studio has given Apple the rights to store and distribute the movie in this manner.

Downloading Podcasts

Podcasts are episodic shows, either audio or video, produced by major networks, small companies, and single individuals. You'll find news, information, tutorials, music, comedy, drama, talk shows, and more. There is something covering almost any topic you can think of.

To subscribe to and listen to or watch podcasts, you need to get the Podcasts app from Apple. You can find it in the App Store and add it to your iPad for free. See "Purchasing an App" in Chapter 15 for a step-by-step on how to get a new app.

1. Tap the Podcasts app icon on your Home screen.

2. Tap the Library button to look at the podcasts you've already downloaded. If you start off by looking at your library, you'll see an equivalent button labeled Catalog at the bottom left that takes you back to this screen.

3. Use the Search field to search for a podcast by name or keyword.

4. Tap a podcast to get more information about it. You can also swipe right to left to view more in the list.

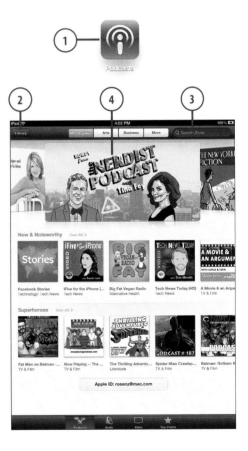

5. Tap Rating and Reviews to see what others have to say.

6. Tap the Download button next to a single episode to download just that episode.

7. Tap Subscribe to subscribe to the podcast. This will download the latest episode and also automatically get new episodes as they become available.

8. Using the Library button from step 2, you can go to the list of podcasts and view them by icon or in a list. Tap the list button to see them as a list with each episode shown on the right.

9. Tap the episode to watch or listen to it. Swipe left to right across an episode to delete it.

10. Tap the info button to get more details about an episode and to mark it as played without listening.

11. Tap the settings button to set the sort order and auto-download preferences for the podcast.

12. Tap Edit to be able to delete podcast subscriptions from your library.

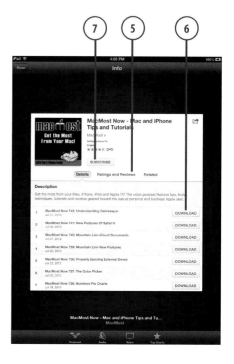

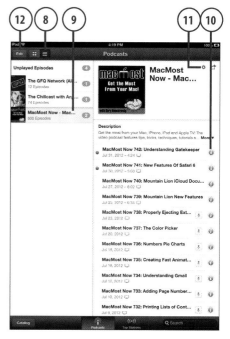

Playing Video

After you have movies, TV shows, and Podcast videos on your iPad, you need to play them using the Videos app.

1. Tap the Videos app icon on your Home screen.

2. The Movies you have on your iPad display by default. Tap TV Shows or Podcasts to switch lists. If you don't have videos in one or more of these categories, then that button may not appear at all.

3. Tap a movie to view more information about it.

Any Video Alternatives to Apple?

You bet. An app for Netflix launched with the iPad that Netflix subscribers can use to stream movies. Amazon also has an Amazon Instant Video app for subscribers to their service. Some companies, such as ABC, have also provided their own apps for viewing their shows on the iPad. You can also view video from any site that has video in standard MP4 formats. The site www.archive.org/details/movies has public domain movies and videos, often in MP4 format. The popular video site http://blip.tv also works well with the iPad.

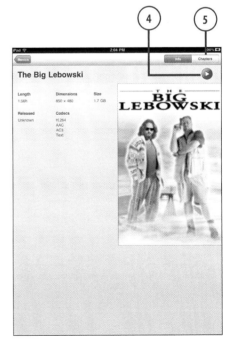

---

4. Tap the Play button to start the movie.

5. Tap the Chapters button to view a list of chapters in the movie.

6. After a movie is playing, tap in the middle of the screen to bring up the controls.

7. Tap the Done button to exit the movie and return to the movie information screen.

8. Tap the Pause button to pause the movie and then again to resume.

9. Adjust the volume with the volume control.

10. Drag the dot along the line to move to a different section of the movie.

11. Use the Back and Forward buttons to jump between chapters.

12. Use the AirPlay button to send the video stream to another device, such as an Apple TV. See "Using AirPlay to Play Music and Video on Other Devices" later in this chapter.

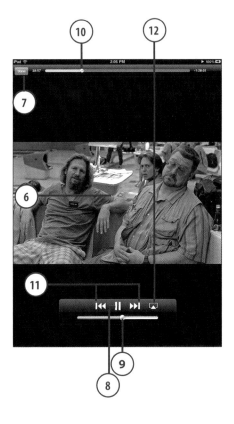

Changing the Orientation

For most video content, you can rotate your iPad to view in a horizontal orientation and use the Zoom button at the upper right to crop the left and right sides of the video so that it fits vertically on the screen. This is similar to watching a movie on a standard TV.

What Happened to the YouTube App?

In iOS 5 and previous versions of iOS, there was a special YouTube app that enabled you to view YouTube videos. In iOS 6 this was removed. But you can still view YouTube videos by using Safari and browsing to http://youtube.com just like you would on a computer. It is also possible that at some point in the future Google may release a new stand-alone YouTube app, so look for it in the App Store.

Using AirPlay to Play Music and Video on Other Devices

In iTunes, with the Video app and many other apps that play music or video, you have the option to send the audio or video stream from your iPad to another device that is connected to the same Wi-Fi network, such as an Apple TV.

You need to enable AirPlay on those devices first. For instance, using the Apple TV (2nd generation models), you need to go into settings on the device and turn on AirPlay. You also need to make sure that the device is using the same Wi-Fi network as your iPad.

1. Look for the AirPlay button in the app you are using. Tap it to bring up a list of available devices.

2. Your iPad will show as the first device. Use this to switch back to playing the media on your iPad if you have switched to something else.

3. Next to each device, you will see either a screen icon or a speaker icon. This tells you whether you can stream video or just audio using that device.

4. Tap on another device, and the music or video currently playing will start to play over that device.

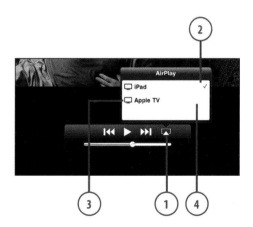

AirPlay Everything

You can also use AirPlay to mirror your iPad's screen with an up-to-date Apple TV 2. Just access the multitask switcher and go all the way to the controls section. (See "Viewing Currently Running Apps" in Chapter 15.) There is an AirPlay button there, too. You can use that to turn on mirroring and send your screen to the Apple TV. Some apps, however, specially block this.

Home Sharing

If you are using iTunes on your Mac or PC, you can play this iTunes content on your iPad if it is on the same local network.

1. In iTunes on your Mac or PC, choose Turn On Home Sharing from the Advanced menu. You are prompted to enter your Apple account ID and password.

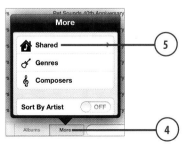

2. In the Settings App, choose Music settings.

3. Enter the same Apple account ID and password.

4. In the Music app, tap the More button at the bottom of the screen.

5. Tap Shared, and then choose the name of the library you want to access. The content in your Music app changes to reflect the content in the iTunes library on your Mac or PC. You can now play songs from your computer without having to transfer them to your iPad first.

What if My Library Doesn't Appear?

Home Sharing is tricky. It requires that you use the same iTunes account IDs on both your iPad and on your Mac or PC. It also requires that you have the iPad on the same local network as your Mac or PC. In addition, network firewalls and other software may get in the way. It usually works effortlessly, but some users have reported trouble getting Home Sharing to work at all with their particular home network setup.

Purchase and read books with the iPad's ebook reader.

Find out how to purchase books from the iBooks store and how to read them on your iPad.

→ Buying a Book from Apple
→ Reading a Book
→ Using Reading Aids
→ Adding Notes and Highlights
→ Adding Bookmarks
→ Organizing Your Books
→ Using iBooks Alternatives

5

Reading Books

We finally have a better way to enjoy books. As an ebook reader, your iPad can give you access to novels and textbooks alike, storing hundreds inside and allowing you to purchase more right from the device.

A single app, the iBooks app, allows you to both read and purchase new books. You can also download and add books from other sources.

Buying a Book from Apple

The first thing to do with the iBooks app is to get some books! You can buy books using the store in the app. You can also find some free books there.

1. Tap the iBooks app icon to launch iBooks.

2. Tap the Store button to switch to the iBooks store.

Don't Want to Purchase from Apple?

You don't necessarily need to buy books from Apple. You can buy from any seller that sends you an ePub or PDF formatted file with no copy protection. After you have the file, just drag and drop it into iTunes. It will add it to your books collection there, ready to be synced to your iPad.

3. Swipe left and right to browse more featured books.

4. Tap Browse to go to a list of book categories.

5. Tap the Charts button to see a list of bestsellers.

6. Swipe up to see more featured categories.

7. Use the search field to search for book titles and authors.

8. Tap any book cover to view more information about the book.

9. Tap the price next to a book to purchase it.

10. The price button changes to Buy Book. Tap it again to continue with the purchase.

11. Tap the Get Sample button to download a sample of the book.

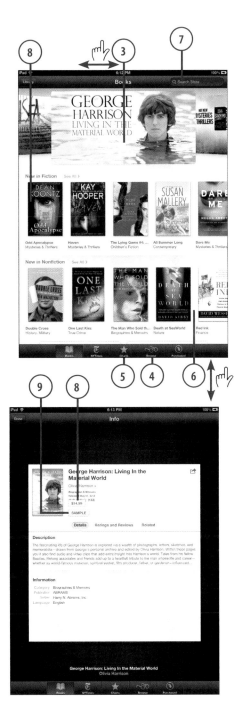

Reading a Book

Reading books is a simple process. Following are the basics of reading your downloaded books.

1. Tap the iBooks app icon to launch iBooks.

2. Tap a book to open it.

Can't Find Your Book?

Did you download a book only to discover that you can't see it in your Library? Try tapping the Collections button at the top of the screen and switching to a different collection. For instance, by default, PDF documents are put in the PDF collection, not in the Books collection.

3. To turn a page, tap and hold anywhere along the right side of the page, and drag to the left. A virtual page turns.

4. Tap and drag from the left to the right or simply tap the left side of the page to turn the page back.

5. To move quickly through pages, tap and drag the small marker at the bottom of the page along the dotted line. Release to jump to a page.

6. Tap the Table of Contents button at the top to view a table of contents.

7. Tap anywhere in the table of contents to jump to that part of the book.

8. Tap the Resume button to return to the page you were previously viewing.

9. Tap the Library button to return to your books. If you return to the book later, you return to the last page you viewed.

Tired of the Special Effects?

If you tire of the page-turning special effect, a quick tap on the right or left side of the screen also turns pages. The effect still shows, but it's quick.

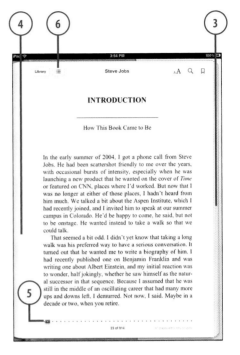

Using Reading Aids

iBooks has a variety of ways you can customize your reading experience. You can change the font size, the font itself, and even turn your iPad on its side to see two pages at one time.

1. While viewing a page in iBooks, tap the display adjustment controls at the top of the screen.

2. Drag the brightness control left or right. Dragging to the left makes the screen dim, which you might use if you're reading in a dark room. Dragging to the right makes it bright, which could make reading easier while outdoors.

3. Tap the smaller "A" button to reduce the size of the text.

4. Tap the larger "A" button to increase the size of the text.

5. Tap the Fonts button to choose from a few font options.

6. Tap the Theme button to select one of the three color themes (White, Sepia, or Night). You can also choose to switch to an all-white background or switch from flipping pages to vertical scrolling.

7. Turn your iPad on its side to change to a two-page view. (Make sure your orientation lock is not on.)

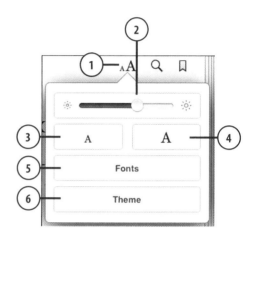

Where Did the Buttons Go?

If you tap in the middle of the screen, the buttons at the top and the dotted line at the bottom disappear. You can still turn the pages; you just don't have access to these buttons. To see the buttons again, tap in the middle of the screen.

Adding Notes and Highlights

Each time you launch iBooks, your iPad returns you to the page you were last reading. However, you might want to mark a favorite passage or a bit of key information.

1. Go to a page in a book in iBooks.

2. Tap a word and hold your finger there for about a second.

3. Release your finger and you see six choices: Copy, Define, Highlight, Note, Search, and Share.

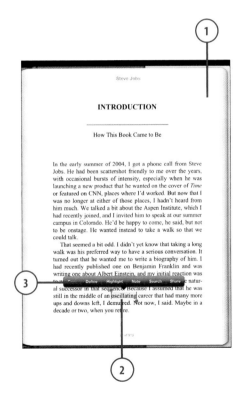

Define and Search

Tapping Define brings up a definition of the word. Tapping Search brings up a list of the locations of the word throughout the text.

Sharing from iBooks

When you choose Share, you can send the excerpt you have selected to someone else using email, a text message, Twitter, or Facebook.

4. Drag the blue dots to enlarge the section of text highlighted.

5. Tap Highlight. Alternatively, you can tap a word and hold for a second and then immediately start dragging to highlight text.

6. The text is now highlighted.

7. Tap the first button to change the type of highlighting. You can choose from various colors or a simple red underline.

8. Tap to remove the highlight completely.

9. Tap Note instead of Highlight to bring up a yellow pad of paper and add a note.

10. Tap in the note to bring up the keyboard and start typing.

11. Tap outside the yellow paper to finish the note. It will then appear as a small yellow sticky note to the right side of the page. Tap it any time you want to view or edit the note. You can delete a note by removing all text in the note.

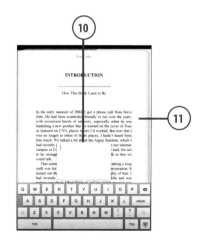

Adding Bookmarks

You can also bookmark a page to easily find it later.

1. Tap the bookmark button at the top of a page to bookmark the page. You can bookmark as many pages as you want in a book.

2. Tap it again to remove the bookmark from the page.

3. Tap the Table of Contents button to go to the table of contents.

4. Tap the Bookmarks button at the top of the table of contents to see a list of all the bookmarks, highlights, and notes you have added to the book.

5. Tap any bookmark, note, or highlight to jump to it.

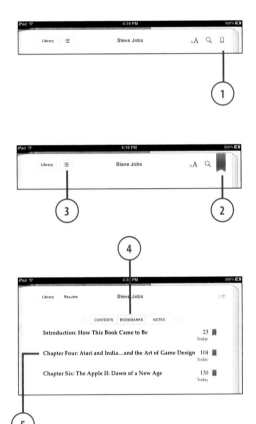

Organizing Your Books

Like to read a lot? You aren't alone. I'm sure many people gather massive collections of ebooks on their iPads. Fortunately, iBooks includes a few great ways to organize your ebooks.

1. Go to your iBooks main page—your Library.

2. Tap the Collections button.

3. Tap a Collection name to jump to that collection. You can think of collections as different bookcases filled with books.

4. Tap New to create a new collection.

5. Tap Edit to delete or re-order collections in the list.

6. Tap the Edit button to enter edit mode.

7. Tap one or more books to select them.

8. Tap the Move button to move those books to another collection.

9. Tap the Delete button to delete those books.

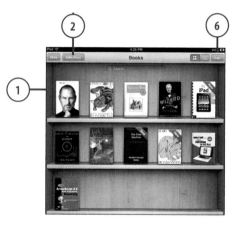

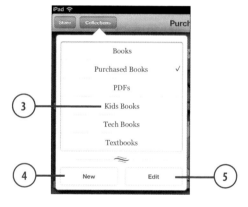

Books in the Cloud

When you view your Purchased Books collection, you will see all of the books you have bought in the past, even if that book is no longer on your iPad because you removed it. These books will have a little iCloud icon in the upper-right corner, and when you select one it will download.

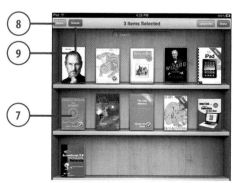

10. Tap and hold your finger over a book to drag it to a new position in the library. You can also do this in normal mode or in edit mode.

11. Tap Done to exit edit mode.

12. Tap the List View button.

13. Now you can see a vertical list of your books. Scroll up and down by dragging and flicking.

14. Tap the Titles, Authors, and Categories buttons at the bottom of the screen to change the order of the list.

15. Use the search field to search your library. If you don't see a search field, tap and drag down on the whole list to reveal it. You can also drag down the screen to reveal the search box in the normal icon view of books and type in a search keyword there.

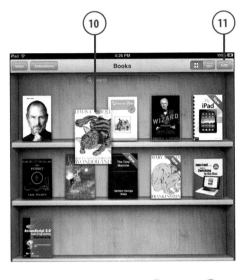

Another Way to Delete

You can also delete books in list view by swiping from left to right across the title of a book. A Delete button appears to the right. Tap it to delete the book.

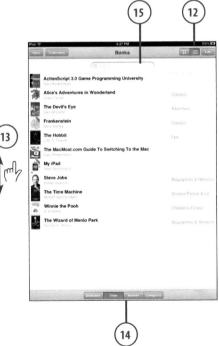

Using iBooks Alternatives

Copy protection prevents you from taking your ebooks from one platform to the other. Thankfully there are Kindle and Nook apps for the iPad, so you can read the books you purchase from those stores.

1. When you launch the Kindle app, you see a screen that displays your library. Tap a book to open it.

2. Tap the middle of the page to bring up controls at the top and bottom.

3. Tap the Font button to change the font size.

4. Tap the right side to flip to the next page.

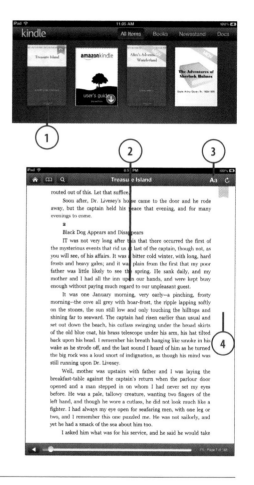

Cloud Versus Device

The new Kindle app has a Cloud/Device control at the bottom of the screen. Selecting Cloud shows you all the books you have purchased. Selecting Device shows you which books are on your iPad and ready to read. You can tap on a book on the Cloud screen to download it to your device. You can tap on it again after it has been downloaded to read it.

More eBook Alternatives

If you like to buy your books from Barnes & Noble, you can also get the Nook app. This lets you read books that can be purchased in the Nook store. If you own a Nook and have already bought books, you can access those books and load them onto your iPad.

Another App you can get is the Google Play Books app. This works with books purchased in the Google Play store, which is similar to the Amazon Kindle store or the iBookstore. You can choose whether you want to buy from Apple, Amazon, Barnes & Noble, or Google.

Track your
appointments
and events.

Set reminders.

Store and
search
all your
contacts.

Take notes
and create
lists.

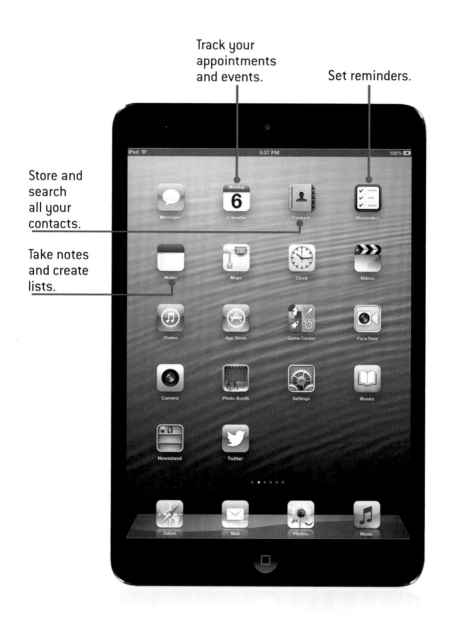

In this chapter, we learn how to add and look up contacts and calendar events. We also look at the Notes app.

Organizing Your Life

Whether you are a well-connected businessperson or just someone who has lots of friends, you can use the iPad to organize your life with the default Contacts and Calendar apps. Let's take a close look at some of the things you can do with these apps.

Adding a Contact

If you use Contacts on your Mac or the equivalent on Windows, all your contacts can transfer to your iPad the first time you sync. However, you can also add contacts directly on your iPad.

1. Tap the Contacts app icon to launch the app.

2. Press the + button near the bottom of the screen. A New Contact form and keyboard appear.

3. Type the first name of the contact. No need to use Shift to capitalize the name because that happens automatically.

4. Tap the return key on the keyboard to advance to the next field.

5. Continue to type data into fields and tap return. Tap return to skip any fields you don't want to fill.

6. Tap Add Photo to add a photo from one of your photo albums.

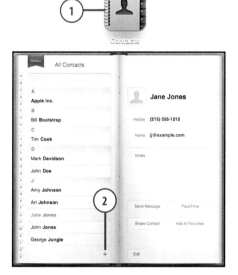

Don't Worry About Formatting

You don't need to type phone numbers with parentheses or dashes. Your iPad formats the number for you.

7. Tap the green + button next to Add New Address to add a physical address to the contact.

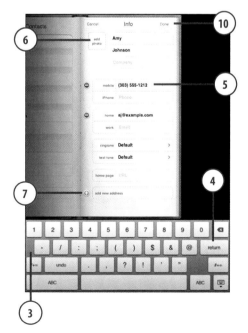

8. Tap the green + button next to Add Field to add a field such as a middle name, job title, birthday, and so on. Note that you may need to scroll down to see the Add Field button.

9. Tap the name of a field you would like to add. Or tap away from the pop-up menu to dismiss it.

10. Tap the Done button to complete the new contact.

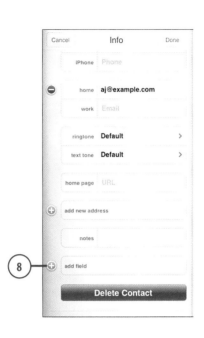

Contacts Sync

Contacts that you add to your iPad sync back to your computer the next time you connect. If you have the iCloud service, the contact should sync across all your iCloud-enabled devices within minutes if your iPad and those devices are connected to the Internet.

 **Siri: Call Me Ray**
You can set a nickname field in a contact. When you do this, and the contact happens to be yours, Siri will call you by that name. You can always tell Siri: "Call me *name*" and it will change your nickname field even if you are not in the Contacts app at the moment.

You can also set relationships in your contacts by saying things like "Debby is my wife."

Searching for a Contact

If you didn't have a lot of friends before, I'm sure you gained quite a few since you became the first on your block to own an iPad. So how do you search though all those contacts to find the one you want?

1. Tap the Contacts app icon to launch the app.

2. Tap in the Search field. A keyboard appears at the bottom of the screen.

Other Ways to Find Contacts

You can also drag (or flick to move quickly) through the contact list to find a name. In addition, the list of letters on the left side of the Contacts app enables you to jump right to that letter in your contacts list.

 Siri: Show Me

You can also use Siri to find a contact. Try these phrases:

"Show me John Smith."
"Show me my contact."
"Show me my wife."

3. Start typing the name of the person you are looking for. As soon as you start typing, the app starts making a list of contacts that contain the letters you've typed.

4. Keep typing until you narrow down the list of names and spot the one you are looking for.

5. Tap the name to bring up the contact.

6. Tap the X button to dismiss the search.

Working with Contacts

After you have contacts in your iPad, you can do a few things from a contact in the Contacts app.

1. Tap and hold the name to copy it to the clipboard buffer.

2. Tap and hold the phone number to copy it to the clipboard buffer.

3. Tap the email address to start composing a new email in the Mail app.

4. Tap to the right of Notes to add more information without entering Edit mode.

5. Tap Edit to enter Edit mode, which gives you the same basic functionality as entering a new contact.

6. Tap Share Contact to start a new email message with a vcard version of the contact.

7. This is the space for an image. To add an image, enter Edit mode by tapping the Edit button at the bottom of the page, and then tapping this space.

8. Tap FaceTime to start a video call (see Chapter 10).

9. Tap Add to Favorites to add to your FaceTime favorites list.

10. Tap Send Message to send a text message to this contact. See "Setting Up Messaging" in Chapter 8.

Creating a Calendar Event

Now that you have people in your Contacts app, you need to schedule some things to do with them. Let's look at the Calendar app.

1. Tap the Calendar app icon on the Home screen.

2. Tap the + button at the bottom right.

3. Enter a title for the event.

4. Enter a Location for the event, or skip this field.

5. Tap the Starts/Ends area to bring up date controls.

6. Drag the day, hour, minute, and AM/PM wheels to set the start time for the event.

7. Tap Ends.

8. Drag the day, hour, minute, and AM/PM wheels to set the end time for the event.

9. If the event is an all-day event, turn on the All-Day switch.

10. Tap Done to complete entering the time for the event.

11. Tap Repeat to select a repeating cycle for the event.

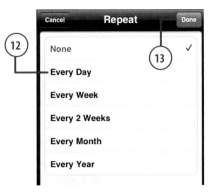

12. Tap the frequency of the event, or leave it at None for a single occurrence.

13. Tap Done to return to the main event screen.

14. Tap Invitees to send an email invitation to another person for this event, if your calendar system allows this.

15. Tap Alert to enter an alert time for the event.

16. Select how much time before the event you want the alert to sound.

17. Tap Done to return to the main event screen.

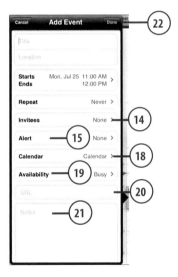

18. If you have more than one calendar, you can place this event in the proper one.

19. You can set your availability to Busy or Free for the event, if your calendar system allows this.

20. You can enter a URL for the event for quick access to a website when the event is shown.

21. Tap in the Notes field and type any additional information for the event.

22. Tap Done to complete the event.

 ### Siri: Creating Events
You can use Siri to create new events even when the Calendar app is not on your screen.

"Schedule a doctor appointment for 3 PM next Wednesday."
"Set up a meeting with John tomorrow at noon."
"Cancel my dentist appointment."

Using Calendar Views

There are four different ways to view your calendar: Day, Week, Month, and List. Let's take a look at each.

Day View

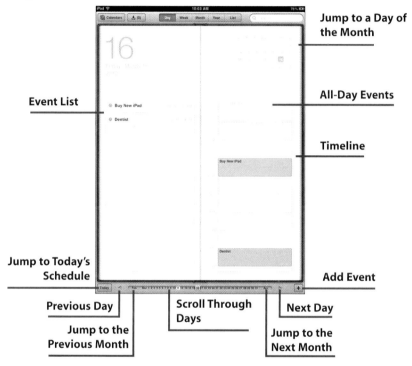

Jump to a Day of the Month

All-Day Events

Timeline

Event List

Jump to Today's Schedule

Add Event

Previous Day

Scroll Through Days

Next Day

Jump to the Previous Month

Jump to the Next Month

The daily view is broken into two halves: a list of the events scheduled for the day and a scrolling area with a block for each half-hour.

You can tap and drag the right area to move up and down in the day. Above that area is a space for all-day events, if there are any.

The month calendar at the upper right enables you to jump to another day in your schedule by tapping a date. You can also choose a date by tapping and sliding the bar at the bottom of the screen, or jump to the previous or next month by tapping the abbreviated month name.

Move one day at a time through the calendar by tapping the arrows at the bottom of the screen. The Today button takes you to the current day's schedule.

You can tap an event on either side of the page to view details and edit it.

Week View

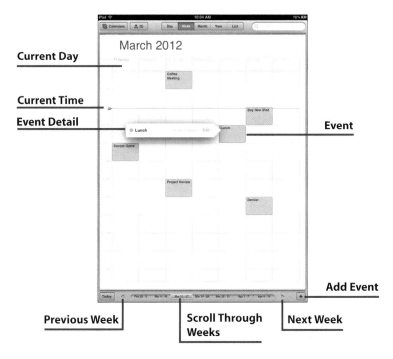

The Week view is a grid. It shows you Sunday through Saturday of the current week. Each event is shown in the grid, and you can tap on one to see its full title, location, and time.

The red dot and line indicates the current time, and the name of the current day is blue at the top of the screen. Use the line at the bottom of the screen to navigate to previous or upcoming weeks.

Month View

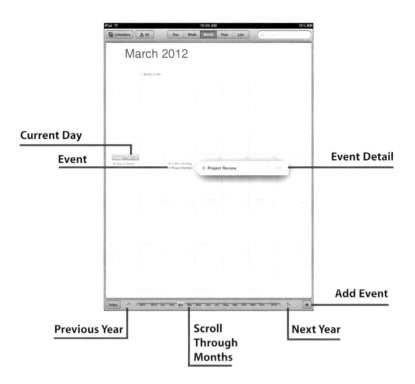

Current Day

Event

Event Detail

Add Event

Previous Year | Scroll Through Months | Next Year

The Month view provides a large view of events. It is still a grid but in a traditional monthly view, with the days from the previous and next months filling in the extra blocks.

Each block lists the events scheduled for that day. You can tap on one to get more information or edit it.

The line at the bottom of the screen changes to a monthly timeline, with previous and next years also listed so that you can jump from year to year.

 ## Siri: Checking Your Schedule

You can use Siri to see what events you have coming up.

"What do I have going on tomorrow?"
"What is on my calendar for this week?"
"When is my dentist appointment?"

List View

Selected Event Information

Event List

Day List

Selected Event

Jump to Today's Schedule

Add Event

Previous Day

Scroll Through Days

Next Day

Jump to the Previous Month

Jump to the Next Month

The List view is an interesting combination of things. On the left, you get a list of all your events, not just the ones for the current day. You can scroll forward even more if you want to see what is coming up.

On the right, you get a daily timeline like the Day view. But instead of a month calendar at the time, you get information about the currently selected event.

Year View

There is also a Year view, as you may have already noticed since there is a Year button at the top of the screen. This shows you 12 very small monthly calendars, with colored-in spaces on days where you have events. You can use this view to quickly navigate to an event in a different week or month. Or, you can use it to see when the days fall in the week.

Creating Notes

Another organization app that comes with your iPad is the Notes app. Although this one is much more free-form than a Contacts or Calendar app, it can be useful for keeping quick notes or to-do lists.

1. Tap the Notes icon on your Home screen.

2. Notes opens up the note you were previously working on. To type, tap on the screen where you want the insertion point, and a keyboard appears.

(1)

What's in a Name

The filename for a note is just the first line of the note, so get in the habit of putting the title of a note as the first line of text to make finding the note easier.

3. To start a new note, tap the + button at the upper right.

4. To view a list of all your notes, and to jump to another note, tap the Notes button.

(4)   **(3)**

iPad

Notes   Daily To-Do List   +

Today   Mar 11 9:58 AM

Daily To-Do List

Go grocery shopping
Clean out inbox   **(2)**
Finish iPad book
Pick up kid from school

5. Tap the name of the note you want to switch to.

6. Tap and type in the Search field to find text inside of notes.

7. Turn your iPad to horizontal orientation, and the Notes button is replaced with a permanent list of notes on the left.

8. Tap the arrow buttons at the bottom of the screen to jump between notes.

9. Tap the Share button at the bottom of the screen to start a new email message in the Mail app using the contents of the note, or to print the note using AirPrint.

10. Tap the Trash button at the bottom to delete notes.

Notes Isn't a Word Processor

You can't actually use Notes for any serious writing. There aren't any styles or formatting choices. You can't even change the display font to make it larger. If you need to use your iPad for writing, consider Pages or a third-party word processing app.

MULTIPLE NOTES ACCOUNTS

What happens to notes after you create them can be confusing. Notes usually are attached to email accounts in the same way email messages are. So creating a new note can make it appear in your email inbox like it is a new message. You can usually adjust what appears in an "inbox" in your email account settings. Sometimes you can specify that you don't want to see notes there. It depends on your email provider.

Setting Reminders

Reminders is a to-do list application available on iPad, iPod touch, iPhone, and Macs running OS X 10.8 Mountain Lion. This app is for creating an ongoing list of tasks you need to accomplish or things you need to remember. These reminders can be similar to calendar events with times and alarms. Or, they can be simple items in a list with no time attached to them.

1. Tap the Reminders icon on your Home screen.

2. Select the list you want to add a new Reminder to.

3. Tap the + button to create a new reminder.

4. Type the new reminder.

5. Type the reminder and close the keyboard when done.

6. Tap the new reminder to bring up the Details dialog.

7. Tap here to edit the reminder.

8. You can also set a reminder time for an alarm.

9. Tap Show More to set a due date, priority, and notes for the reminder.

10. Tap Delete to remove the reminder.

11. Tap outside of the Details box when you are finished editing the reminder.

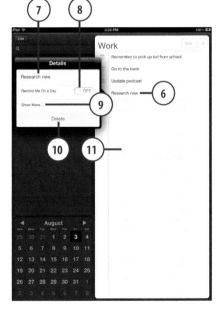

12. Tap the box next to the reminder when you have completed the task. It will remain in the list temporarily.

13. Tap Create New List to add a new reminders list.

14. Tap Completed to see completed reminders.

15. You can also search for reminders by title or content.

16. The mini calendar enables you to look for reminders by date.

17. You can tap Edit to remove reminder lists.

18. Swipe left to right across a reminder to delete it.

Reminders sync by using the iCloud service from Apple. So, they are automatically backed up and should also appear on your Mac in the Reminders app, if you have OS X 10.8 Mountain Lion. And if you use an iPhone, they should appear there as well.

Siri: Remind Me
You can create new reminders using Siri like this:

"Remind me to watch Doctor Who tonight at 8 PM."
"Remind me to pick up milk when I leave work."
"Remind me to check my stocks every day at 9 AM."

Setting Clock Alarms

The Clock app is new for iOS 6 on the iPad, and it can also be used to set alarms. The advantage of using an alarm rather than a reminder is that an often-recurring alarm, like your morning wake-up call, or a reminder on when to pick up your child at school, won't clutter up your Reminders list or calendar.

1. Tap the Clock app.

2. The main screen shows up to six clocks in any time zone you want. Tap a clock to have it fill the screen.

3. Tap an empty clock to add a new city.

4. Tap Edit to remove or rearrange the clocks.

5. Tap Alarm to view and edit alarms.

6. To add a new alarm, tap the + button.

7. Select the days of the week for the alarm.

8. Set a sound for the alarm. You can choose from preset sounds or your ringtone collection.

9. Leave snooze on if you want the ability to use snooze when the alarm goes off.

10. You can give the alarm a custom name.

11. Set a time for the alarm.

12. Tap Save to save all your settings and add the alarm.

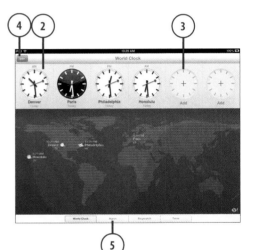

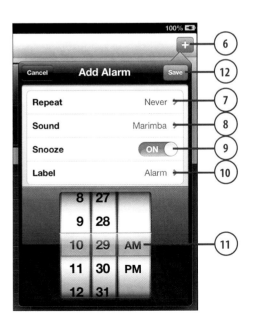

13. The alarm now appears in the special Clock calendar.

14. You can switch off the alarm, while leaving it in the calendar for future use.

15. You can choose an alarm to edit or delete it.

16. The alarm will sound and a message will appear when it is time. Even if your iPad is sleeping, it will wake up.

17. If you've enabled snooze, tapping here will silence the alarm and try again in 9 minutes.

18. To silence the alarm normally, assuming it has sounded while the iPad is asleep and locked, you need to swipe the lock switch. If the iPad was awake when the alarm went off, you simply get a button to tap.

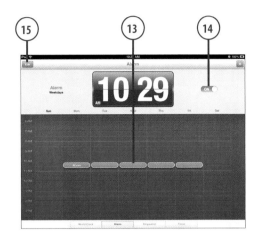

 Siri: Create Alarms

You can use Siri to create and delete alarms. Try these phrases:

"Set an alarm for weekdays at 9 AM."
"Create an alarm for tomorrow at 10 AM."
"Cancel my 9 AM alarm."
"Turn on my 9 AM alarm."
"Turn off my 9 AM alarm."

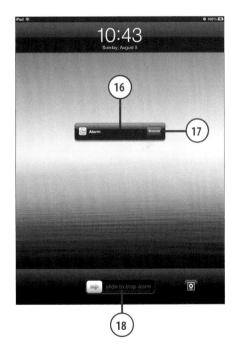

The Web is at your fingertips
with iPad's Safari web browser.

In this chapter, you learn about Safari, the browser built-in to the iPad. You can use it to browse the Web, bookmark web pages, fill in forms, and search the Internet.

Surfing the Web

The iPad is a beautiful web surfing device. Its size is perfect for web pages, and your ability to touch the screen lets you interact with content in a way that even a computer typically cannot.

If you have been using the iPhone or the iPod touch to browse the Web, you immediately notice how you no longer have to pinch and rotate to read text or see links. The screen size is much more ideal for web pages than a mobile phone device.

Browsing to a URL

Undoubtedly, you know how to get to web pages on a computer using a web browser. You use Safari on your iPad in the same way, but the interface is a little different.

At the top of the Safari browser is a toolbar with just a few buttons. In the middle, the largest interface element is the address field. This is where you can type the address of any web page on the Internet.

1. Touch the Safari icon on your iPad to launch the browser. It might be located at the bottom of the screen, along with your other most commonly used applications.

2. Tap in the address field at the top of the screen. This opens up the keyboard at the bottom of the screen. If you were already viewing a web page, the address of that page remains in the address field. Otherwise, it will be blank.

Clear the Slate

To clear the field at any time, tap the X button located inside the field all the way to the right.

3. Start typing a URL such as apple.com or macmost.com.

4. As you type, suggestions based on previous pages you have visited appear. To go directly to one of these pages, tap the page's address in the list.

5. Tap the Go button on the keyboard when you finish typing.

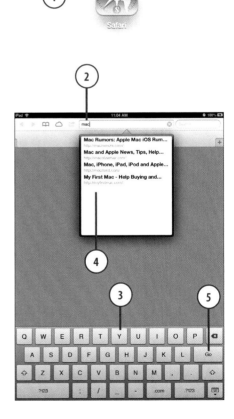

TIPS FOR TYPING A URL

- A URL is a Universal Resource Locator. It can be a website name or a specific page in a website.

- For most websites, you don't need to type the "www." at the beginning. For instance, you can type **www.apple.com** or **apple.com** and both take you to Apple's home page. You never need to type "http://" either, though occasionally you need to type "https://" to specify that you want to go to a secure web page.

- Instead of typing ".com." you can tap the .com button on the iPad keyboard. If you tap and hold the .com button, you can select .edu, .org, .us, or .net as well.

Nothing Special, Please

Some websites present you with a special iPad version of the site. This is not as common as the special iPhone or iPod touch versions that many sites offer. If a website does not look the same on your iPad as it does on your computer, you might want to check to see if a switch is on the web page provided by the site to view the standard web version, instead of a special iPad version. This is especially useful if a site has lumped the iPad together with the iPhone and provided a needlessly simplified version.

Searching the Web

The Web wouldn't be useful if you had to already know the exact location of every web page to view it. The iPad's Safari web browser has search built into it, as a field right at the top of the screen.

As you type, Safari suggests search terms based on previous searches that others have performed starting with the same characters. This list, which changes as you type, can save you a lot of time and even help you better define what you are looking for.

1. Open Safari and tap in the search field at the upper-right portion. It expands, shrinking the address field to give it more room. The keyboard pops up at the bottom of the screen.

2. Start typing your search term.

3. As you type, a pop-up list appears with suggestions. You can stop typing at any time and tap one of these suggestions to select it and start the search.

4. Tap the X button to the right of the search field at any time to clear the field. If you previously searched for something, it might have appeared in the field when you started your search, and you can use the X button to clear that text.

5. Tap the Search button on the keyboard to finish the text entry and start the search.

6. The results display in a typical Google search results page, provided you have Google selected as your search engine. Tap any link to go to a page, or use the links at the bottom of the screen to view more results.

Search This Page

Below Google Suggestions in the search suggestions drop-down menu is a list of recent searches and the occurrences of the phrase on the web page you are viewing. Use the latter to find the phrase on the page.

TIPS FOR SEARCHING THE WEB

You can go deeper than just typing some words. For instance, you can put a + in front of a word to require it and a – in front to avoid that word in the results.

You can use special search terms to look for things such as movie times, weather, flight tracking, and more. See http://www.google.com/landing/searchtips/ for all sorts of things you can do with a Google search.

Using iPad's Settings app, you can choose the search engine that Safari uses as its default. Tap the Settings icon and choose Safari on the left, and then look for the Search Engine setting. You can choose Bing or Yahoo! instead of Google, for instance.

Using Google, you can search for much more than text on web pages. Look at the top of the search results, and you see links such as Images, Videos, Maps, News, and Shopping. Tap "more" and you can also search for things such as Blogs and Books.

To explore the search results without moving away from the page listing the results, tap and hold over a link to see a button that enables you to open a link in a new page, leaving the results open in the current page.

You can use many search settings with Google. These are not specific to the iPad but work on your computer as well when performing searches. Tap the Search Settings link in the upper-right corner of the search results page to choose a language, filters, and other settings. Set up a Google account (same as a Gmail account) and log in to save these search preferences and use them between different devices.

 ## Siri: Search the Web

You can use Siri to search the web, even if you are not currently looking at the Safari screen. Sometimes Siri will also answer general questions by suggesting a web search:

"Search the web for iPad tutorials."
"Search for local plumbers."
"Search for MacMost.com."
"Search Wikipedia for Paris."
"Show me some web sites about geology."
"Google Denver news."
"Search for iPad tutorials on MacMost.com."

Viewing Web Pages

Whether you typed in a URL or searched for a web page, after you have one open on your iPad screen, you can control what you view in several ways. You need to know these techniques to view the complete contents of a web page and navigate among web pages.

1. Navigate to any web page using either of the two techniques in the previous step-by-step instructions.

2. When you are viewing a page, you can touch and drag the page up and down with your finger. As you do so, notice the bar on the right side that gives you an indication of how much of the complete web page you are viewing at one time.

Flick It

If you release your finger from the iPad screen to stop scrolling while dragging, the screen will continue to scroll with a decelerating affect and then come to a stop quickly.

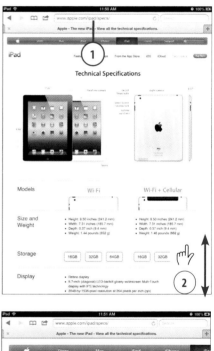

3. To zoom in on an area in the page, touch the screen with two fingers and move your fingers apart. This is called an unpinch. You can also move them closer together (pinch) to zoom back out. A double-tap restores the page to normal scaling. This works well on websites made for desktop computers, but mobile sites usually are set to already fit the screen at optimal resolution.

4. You can also double-tap images and paragraphs of text to zoom in to those elements in the web page. A second double-tap zooms back out.

5. While zoomed in, you can also touch and drag left and right to view different parts of the web page. You see a bar at the bottom of the screen when you do this, just like the bar on the right side in step 2.

6. To move to another web page from a link in the current web page, just tap the link. Links are usually an underlined or colored piece of text; however, they can also be pictures or button-like images.

It's Not All Good

WHERE'S THE LINK?

Unfortunately, it isn't always easy to figure out which words on a page are links. Years ago, these were all blue and underlined. But today, links can be any color and may not be underlined.

On the iPad, it is even more difficult to figure out which words are links. This is because many web pages highlight links when the cursor moves over the word. But with the touch interface of the iPad, there is no cursor.

Returning to Previously Visited Websites

Returning to the last page you visited is easy. Just tap the Back button, which is the left-facing triangle at the top-left corner of the Safari screen. You can continue to tap the Back button to go to pages you visited previously.

Likewise, you can tap the button next to it, the Forward button, to reverse your direction and move forward, returning to your more recently viewed pages.

A more precise way to view previous pages is to use the History button.

1. After using Safari to view several pages, tap the Bookmarks/History button at the top of the screen.

2. Tap the History button to view your browsing history as opposed to your bookmarks or reading list. A list of pages that you visited today appears.

3. Tap any item in the list to jump to that web page.

4. If you visited many sites today, Earlier Today appears and below that, previous days may also appear. Tap to dig down into the history for that date.

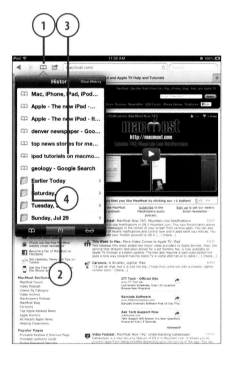

5. When you are into the history for a specific date, you can tap and drag to scroll up and down on longer lists, or tap an item to jump to that page.

6. You can move back up from a specific date to the main History menu by tapping the History button at the top-left part of the History pop-up menu.

History/Bookmarks

Safari treats both History and Bookmarks the same. They are both just lists of web pages. Think of your history as a bookmark list of every site you have visited recently.

TIPS FOR USING HISTORY

- You can clear your history at any time by tapping the Clear History button at the top of the History pop-up menu.

- You can close the History pop-up menu by tapping the History button again or tapping anywhere else on the screen away from the History pop-up menu.

- If you have many items in your history for today, you get an Earlier Today item listed just above previous date items. Tap this to view all the web pages you visited today.

- If you tap the Bookmarks button at the top of the History pop-up menu, you can go up a level and see both Bookmarks and a menu item to take you back to your history.

Bookmarking Websites

While using Safari on the iPad, you need to bookmark some of the sites you visit most often. This can give you quick access to the information you need the most.

1. Use Safari to navigate to any web page.

2. Tap the Share button at the top of the screen.

3. Choose Bookmark.

4. Edit the title of the bookmark. The official title of the web page is prefilled, but you can use the keyboard to change it. You can tap the X to clear the text and start fresh.

Print It

You'll also notice the Print button when you tap the same button you use to create bookmarks. If you are using a printer compatible with Apple's AirPlay technology in your iPad, you can send the current page to a printer attached to your network. See "Printing from Your iPad" in Chapter 18 for details.

5. Tap the Bookmarks folder name to select a folder to place the bookmark.

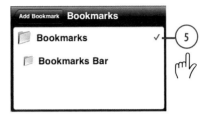

TIPS FOR BOOKMARKING WEBSITES

- You can save bookmarks to a folder called the Bookmarks Bar. These appear as buttons at the top of your browser. Only save the most important bookmarks to the Bookmarks Bar folder. These always show up at the top of your Safari screen.

- The titles of web pages are often long and descriptive. It is a good idea to shorten the title to something you can easily recognize, especially if it is a web page that you plan to visit often. Shorter names also save space in the bookmarks bar.

- You can create folders of bookmarks in your Bookmarks Bar folder. These appear as their own pop-up menu when you tap them, giving you direct access to a subset of your bookmarks.

Reading Lists

You can also put bookmarks into a special Reading List using the Add to Reading List button. This is a good way to temporarily bookmark a page you want to revisit one more time. The Reading List is like your Bookmarks, and you can get to it in the same place. But it is just a simple list of pages without subfolders. It is also possible to view All or only Unread items in the list. So after checking out the page a second time from your Reading List, it will no longer appear as Unread.

Deleting Your Bookmarks

Adding and using bookmarks is just the start. You eventually need to delete ones you don't use. You might find that over time you no longer need some bookmarks. Some might even link to missing or obsolete pages. There are two ways to delete a bookmark. The results of the two methods are the same; however, you might find the second method gives you a little more control.

Delete a Single Bookmark

The first method uses the Bookmarks list to locate and delete a single bookmark.

1. Tap the Bookmarks/History button at the top of the Safari screen.

2. Tap Bookmarks.

3. Swipe across a bookmark, from left to right, with your finger. This brings up a red Delete button.

4. Tap the Delete button to remove the bookmark. The bookmark is instantly deleted.

Another Way to Delete Bookmarks

This method for deleting bookmarks lets you unlock and delete bookmarks from the Bookmarks list.

1. Tap the Bookmarks/History button at the top of the Safari screen.

2. Tap Bookmarks.

3. Tap the Edit button at the upper-right corner. (It becomes the Done button.) Now each bookmark has a red circle with a line through it to its left.

4. Tap one of the red circles to unlock it. A Delete button appears to the right.

5. Tap the Delete button to remove the bookmark.

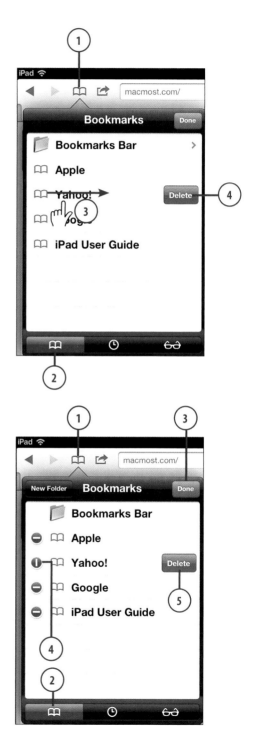

Sync Your Bookmarks

If you want to go to town and really organize your bookmarks, you might be better off doing so on your Mac or PC with the Safari browser. Syncing your iPad to your computer should sync your bookmarks as well. And if you are using iCloud, the syncing should be immediate and automatic. Safari on your computer gives you greater control over moving and deleting bookmarks. So just do your wholesale editing on your computer and resync.

Creating Home Screen Bookmarks

If a web page is somewhat important, you might want to create a bookmark for it. If it is extremely important and you need to go to it often, you might want to make sure that bookmark is saved to your Bookmarks Bar so that it is easily accessible.

However, if a web page is even more important to you than that, you can save it as an icon on your iPad's Home screen.

1. Use Safari to navigate to any web page.

2. Tap the boxed arrow button at the top of the screen.

3. Choose Add to Home Screen. Note that the icon shown here will change to use the icon for that website or a small screen capture of the site.

Managing Home Screen Bookmarks

You can arrange and delete Home screen bookmarks just like icons that represent apps. See "Arranging Apps on Your iPad" in Chapter 15 for details.

4. You can now edit the name of the page. Most web page titles are too long to display under an icon on the Home screen of the iPad, so edit the name down to as short a title as possible.

5. You can tap Cancel to leave this interface without sending the bookmark to the Home screen.

6. Tap Add to complete adding the icon to the Home screen.

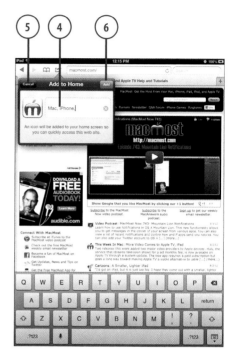

Website Icons

The icon for this type of book-mark can come from one of two sources. Web page owners can provide a special iPhone/iPad icon that would be used whenever someone tries to bookmark her page.

However, if no such icon has been provided, your iPad can take a screen shot of the web page and shrink it down to make an icon.

Building a Reading List

Your reading list is similar to bookmarks. You can add a page to your reading list to remember to return to that page later. When you do, it will be removed from the Unread section of your reading list, but still appear in the All section.

In addition, pages you add to your reading list are downloaded to your iPad so that you can read them later while not connected to the Internet.

1. Find an article you want to read later.

2. Tap the Share button.

3. Tap Add to Reading List.

4. To see your reading list, tap the Bookmarks/History button.

5. Tap the Reading List button.

6. You can tap here to see a list of pages you have added to your reading list, but have not yet viewed.

7. After you have viewed a page, it is removed from the Unread section, but you can still find it in the All section. Tap All to view that list. To remove any article completely, swipe right to left across any item and tap Delete.

8. Tap the item to view the article.

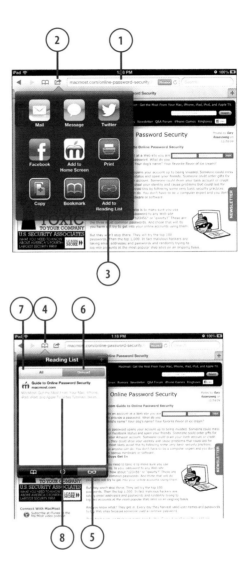

Filling in Web Forms

The Web isn't a one-way street. Often you need to interact with web pages, filling in forms or text fields. Doing this on the iPad is similar to doing it on a computer, but with notable differences.

The keyboard shares screen space with the web page, so when you tap on a field, you bring up the keyboard at the bottom of the screen.

Also pull-down menus behave differently. On the iPad, you get a special menu showing you all the options.

1. Use Safari to navigate to a web page with a form. For demonstration purposes, try one of the pages at http://apple.com/feedback/.

2. To type in a text field, tap that field.

3. The keyboard appears at the bottom of the screen. Use it to type text into the field.

4. Tap the Go button when you finish.

5. To select a check box or radio button, tap it just as you would click on it on your computer using the mouse.

6. To select an item in a pull-down menu, tap the menu.

7. The special iPad pull-down menu reacts like any other iPad interface. You can tap an item to select it. You can touch and drag up and down to view more selections if the list is long.

8. A check mark appears next to the currently selected item. Tap that item or any other one to select it and dismiss the menu.

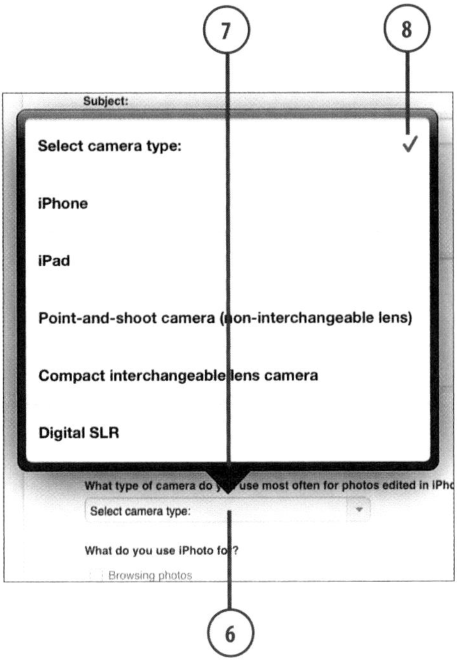

Special Menus

Some websites may use special menus that they build from scratch, rather than these default HTML menus. When this is the case, you get a menu that looks exactly like the one you get when viewing the web page on a computer. If the web page is well coded, it should work fine on the iPad, though it might be slightly more difficult to make a selection.

7

8

Subject:

Select camera type: ✓

iPhone

iPad

Point-and-shoot camera (non-interchangeable lens)

Compact interchangeable lens camera

Digital SLR

What type of camera do you use most often for photos edited in iPho

Select camera type: ▾

What do you use iPhoto for?

Browsing photos

6

TIPS FOR FILLING IN FORMS

- You can use the AutoFill button just above the keyboard to fill in your name, address, and other contact info instead of typing on the keyboard. To enable AutoFill, go into your iPad Settings and look for the AutoFill preferences under Safari. Also make sure your own information is correct and complete in your card in the Contacts application.

- To move between fields in a form, use the Previous and Next buttons just above the keyboard. You can quickly fill in an entire form this way without having to tap on the web page to select the next item.

Opening Multiple Web Pages

Safari on the iPad enables you to open multiple web pages at the same time. You can view only one at a time, but you can hold your place on a page while you look at something on another page.

Previously on the iPad, you used a complex system of pages to do this. But in iOS version 5, you can use tabbed browsing just as you can on Mac and PC browsers.

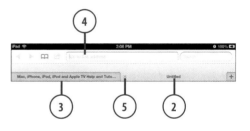

1. While browsing the Web using Safari on the iPad, tap the + button at the top of the screen to the right.

2. You see two tabs at the top of the screen now. The one on the right is in front of the one on the left and is labeled Untitled since no page has yet been loaded. You can see that no web page is displayed below the tabs.

3. You can return to the previous tab by tapping it.

4. You can enter a web address to load a page in this tab. Alternatively, you can enter a search term or use a bookmark to navigate to a web page.

5. You can close the current tab by tapping the X button to the right of the tab's name.

iCloud Tabs

If you have iCloud set up on multiple iOS 6 devices and/or Macs running Mountain Lion, you may see a cloud icon in the Safari toolbar next to the Share button. Tap that and you will see tabs that are currently open on those other devices. You can select one item to open that page. This means you can surf on your Mac for a while, and then switch to the iPad and easily find the pages you were just looking at on your Mac.

TIPS FOR USING MULTIPLE WEB PAGES

- Another way to open up a second page is to tap and hold a link. Then you get a pop-up menu with the option to open the link in a new tab.

- Using multiple pages is yet another way, besides bookmarks, to quickly access the same web page over and over again. Simply start a new tab instead of navigating away from the current page altogether. Then switch tabs to quickly revisit the original page.

Copying Text and Images from Web Pages

You can select text from web pages to copy and paste into your own documents or email messages.

1. Use Safari to navigate to a web page.

2. Tap and hold over a piece of text. You don't need to be exact because you can adjust the selection later. The word Copy appears above the selected area that is highlighted in light blue.

3. You can tap and drag one of the four blue dots to change the selection area. When your selection gets small enough, it changes to only two blue dots indicating the first and last character of the selection.

4. Tap outside the selection to cancel at any time.

5. Tap the Copy button over the selection to copy the text.

6. You can now go to another application such as Mail or Pages and tap in a text area to choose Paste and paste the text into the area. You can also do this in a form on a page in Safari, such as a web-based email form.

Using Images from Web Pages

Along with copying and pasting text from Safari, you can copy images and save them to your photo collection.

1. Use Safari to navigate to a web page that has an image you want to save.

2. Tap and hold your finger on that image.

3. Select Save Image. This saves your image to your Saved Images folder in the Photos app. You can then use this image in any app where you select images from your photo albums.

4. Select Copy to copy the image to the Clipboard. You can then go to a program such as Mail or Pages and paste that image into the document you are composing.

Viewing News Articles with Safari Reader

Web pages on the iPad can be vibrant and pretty. But sometimes the website tries to cram so much text and other junk onto a page that it can be painful to read. You can clear away all the clutter to reveal the text of a news article or blog post using the Reader feature.

1. Look for the Reader button in the address field. It will only appear on some news articles and blog posts. Tap it to enter the Reader mode.

2. In Reader mode, only the text and inline images of the article appear.

3. Tap the font size button to increase or decrease the size of the text.

4. Tap Reader again to return to the regular view of the page.

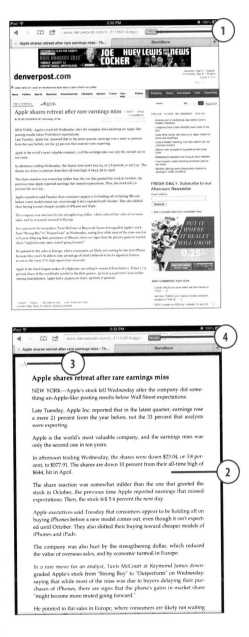

Send and receive
messages from other
iOS and Mac users.

Keep up
with your
friends on
Twitter.

Send and receive email from your ISP
or a variety of popular email services.

Next, we look at how to configure and use the Mail program on your iPad to correspond using email and how to use the Messaging and Twitter apps to send and receive messages.

8

Communicating with Email, Messaging, and Twitter

Now that you have a take-anywhere iPad with a battery that seems to last forever, you have no excuse for not replying to emails, so you need to be comfortable using the built-in Mail app that enables you to connect with your home or work email using standard protocols such as POP and IMAP. You can even connect with more proprietary systems such as AOL, Exchange, and Yahoo!.

Configuring Your Email

Here is a complete list of what information you need to set up your iPad for a traditional email account. If you have a service such as Exchange, Gmail, AOL, Yahoo!, or iCloud, you won't need all this.

- Email Address

- Account Type (POP or IMAP)

- Incoming Mail Server Address

- Incoming Mail User ID

- Incoming Mail Password

- Outgoing Mail Server Address

- Outgoing Mail User ID

- Outgoing Mail Password

IMAP VERSUS POP

POP (Post Office Protocol) fetches and removes email from a server. The server acts as a temporary holding place for email. It is difficult to use POP if you receive email using both your iPad and a computer. You need to either deal with some email going to one device and some to another or set up one device to not remove email from the server so that the other device can retrieve it as well.

IMAP (Internet Message Access Protocol) makes the server the place where all messages are stored, and your iPad and computer simply display what is on the server. It is more ideal in situations where you have multiple devices getting email from the same account.

If you wonder why you shouldn't skip all the setup and just use webmail on your iPad, it's because you can't use emailing features in other apps—such as emailing web page links or emailing photos—if you don't configure the email settings.

1. Tap the Settings icon on your Home screen.

2. Tap Mail, Contacts, Calendars.

3. Tap Add Account.

4. If you have an iCloud, Microsoft Exchange, Gmail, Yahoo! Mail, AOL, or Hotmail account, tap the corresponding button. From there, simply enter your information, and your iPad figures out the rest. You can skip the rest of the steps!

5. Tap Other if you have a traditional POP or IMAP account from work, your Internet providers, or a traditional hosting company.

6. Tap Add Mail Account.

7. Tap in the Name field and enter your name.

8. Tap in the Address field and enter your email address.

9. Tap in the Password field and enter your password.

10. The Description field should automatically fill with a copy of your email address. Keep it or use another description for the account.

11. Tap Save.

12. Tap IMAP or POP as the email account type.

13. Tap in the Incoming Mail Server, Host Name field and enter your email host's address.

14. Tap in the Incoming Mail Server, User Name field and enter your user name.

15. Tap in the Incoming Mail Server, Password field and enter your password.

16. Repeat the previous three steps for Outgoing Mail Server.

17. Tap Save, and the verification process, which can take up to a minute, begins.

What if the Settings Won't Verify?

If your settings fail to verify, you need to double-check all the information you entered. When something is wrong, it often comes down to a single character being mistyped in one of these fields.

Reading Your Email

You use the Mail app to read your email, which is much easier to navigate and type in horizontal mode. Let's start by reading some email.

1. Tap the Mail app icon on the Home screen.

2. On the left, you see a list of incoming mail. On the right, you see the selected message.

3. Tap a message to view it.

4. If you want to check for new mail, drag the list of messages down and release. It will spring back up and ask the server to see if there are new messages.

5. Tap the Details button to see more fields, such as To: and Cc: email addresses.

6. Tap the email address of the sender.

7. Tap Create New Contact to add the sender to your contacts.

8. Tap Add to Existing Contact to add the email address to a contact you already have in your Contacts app.

9. Tap the Folder button at the top of the message.

10. Tap a folder to move the current message to that folder.

11. Tap the Trash button at the top of the message to send the message directly to the Trash folder.

12. Tap the arrow button at the top of the message to reply or forward the message.

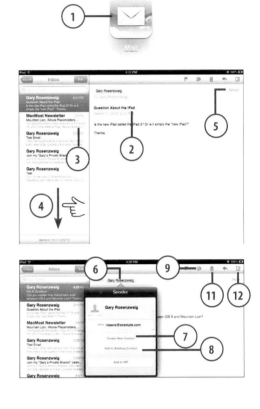

Multiple Inboxes

If you have more than one email account, you can choose to look at each inbox individually or a single unified inbox that includes messages from all accounts. Just tap the Mailboxes button at the upper-left corner of the screen and choose All Inboxes. You can also choose to look at the inbox of a single account, or dig down into any folder of an account.

How Do You Create Folders?

For most email accounts—particularly IMAP, Gmail, and iCloud accounts—you can create mailboxes using the Mail app. Use the back arrow at the upper-left corner of Mail and back out to the list of inboxes and accounts. Choose an account. Then tap the Edit button, and you'll see a New Mailbox button at the bottom of the screen.

VIPs

New in iOS 6 is the ability to make a contact a "VIP." You can do that when you select the sender's name in an incoming email. Then their messages will continue to appear in your inbox as normal, but they will also appear in the VIP inbox. So if you get a lot of email and want to occasionally focus only on a few very important people instead of everyone, choose your VIP inbox rather than your inbox.

If you are using VIPs with your iCloud email accounts, you'll see the same VIPs for your Mac and other iOS devices using that iCloud account.

Composing a New Message

Whether you compose a new message or reply to one you received, the process is similar. Let's take a look at composing one from scratch.

1. In the Mail app, tap the Compose button.

2. Enter a To: address.

3. Alternatively, tap the + button to bring up a list of contacts, and choose from there.

4. Tap in the Subject field and type a subject for the email.

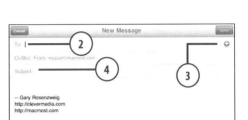

Siri: Sending Email

You can use Siri to send email by asking it to "send an email to" and the name of the recipient. It will ask you for a subject and a body to the message, and then display it. You can choose to send it or cancel.

5. Tap below the subject field in the body of the email, and type your message.

6. Tap the Send button.

Including Images

You can copy and paste inside a Mail message just like you can inside of any text entry area on your iPad. But you can also paste in images! Just copy an image from any source—Photos app, Safari, and so on. Then tap in the message body and select Paste. You can paste in more than one image as well.

Creating a Signature

You can create a signature that appears below your messages automatically. You do this in the Settings app.

1. In the Settings app, choose Mail, Contacts, Calendars.

2. Tap Signature, which is way down in the list on the right.

3. If you have more than one email account set up, you can choose to have one signature for all accounts or a different signature for each account.

4. Type a signature in one of the signature text fields. You don't need to do anything to save the signature. You can tap the Home button on your iPad to exit Settings if you like.

Case-By-Case Signatures

You can have only one signature, even if you have multiple email accounts on your iPad. But the signature is placed in the editable area of the message composition field, so you can edit it like the rest of your message.

Deleting and Moving Messages

While viewing a message you can simply tap the Trash Can icon and move it to the trash. You can also move a group of messages to a folder or the trash.

1. In the Mail app, go to any mailbox and any subfolder, such as your Inbox.

2. Tap the Edit button.

3. Tap the circles next to each message to select them. They will be added to the middle of the screen in a slightly messy stack.

4. Tap the Delete button to delete the selected messages.

5. Tap the Move button, and the left side of the screen changes to a list of folders. You can select one to move all the messages to that folder.

6. Tap the Cancel button to exit without deleting or moving any messages.

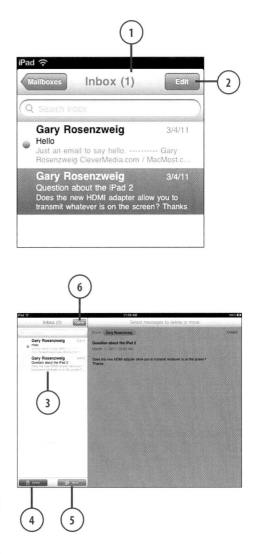

What About Spam?

Your iPad has no built-in spam filter. Fortunately, most email servers filter out spam at the server level. Using a raw POP or IMAP account from an ISP might mean you don't have any server-side spam filtering, unfortunately. But using an account at a service such as Gmail means that you get spam filtering on the server and junk mail automatically goes to the Junk folder, not your Inbox.

Searching Email

You can also search your messages using the Mail app.

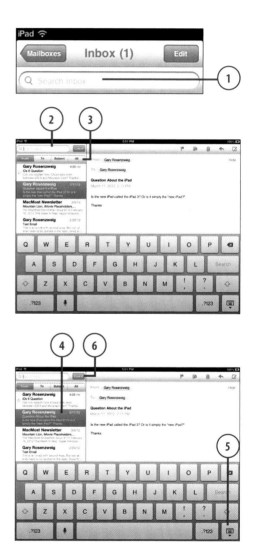

1. In the Mail app, from a mailbox view, tap the Search field.

2. Type a search term.

3. Select From, To, Subject, or All to decide which part of the messages to search.

4. Select a message to view from the search results.

5. Tap the keyboard hide key at the bottom right to hide the keyboard.

6. Tap Cancel to exit the search and return to the mailbox you were previously viewing.

Searching Text Inside Messages

Searches work on From, To, and Subject fields. You can also search the body of your messages by selecting the All option. However, this only works on messages stored on your iPad. If you are using a server-based email solution, such as IMAP, iCloud, Gmail, an so on, you may not get all the results you expect.

Configuring How Email Is Received

You have more settings for email beyond the basic account setup. You can decide how you want to receive email, using either push delivery (iCloud and Microsoft Exchange) or fetch delivery (all other email accounts).

1. Go to the Settings app and tap on Mail, Contacts, Calendars.

2. Tap Fetch New Data.

3. Turn on Push to use push email reception if you use email accounts that can send email via push.

4. Otherwise, select how often you want your iPad to go out to the server and fetch email.

5. Tap Advanced.

6. For each account using fetch, tap the account to turn Fetch to Fetch or Manual.

Push Settings

The two choices for most email accounts are Fetch and Manual. If you have a push account, such as iCloud, you have three choices: Push, Fetch, and Manual. You can switch a Push account to Fetch or Manual if you prefer.

 Siri: Checking Email

You can ask Siri for a quick list of new email messages by saying "check my email." You'll get a list from within the Siri interface, and you can tap on a message to read it in the Mail app.

More Email Settings

You can change even more email settings in the Settings app. Let's take a look at some of them.

1. Tap Show to choose the number of messages to show in your Inbox. You can choose 25, 50, 75, 100, or 200.

2. Tap Preview to choose how many lines of message preview to show when stacking messages up in the list view.

3. Turn Show To/Cc Label on to view "To" or "Cc" in each email listed so that you know if you were the primary recipient or someone who was just copied on an email to someone else.

4. Turn Ask Before Deleting on to require a confirmation when you tap the trash can button in Mail.

5. Turn Load Remote Images off so that images referenced in an mail but stored on a remote server are not shown in the message body.

6. To group replies to a message under the original message, select Organize By Thread. This is handy when you subscribe to email discussion lists.

7. Turn Always Bcc Myself on if you want to get a copy of every email you send so that later you can move your copies of emails to your Sent folder on your computer.

8. Choose whether to indent the quoted text from the original email when replying to a message.

9. Tap Default Account to determine which account is used to send email by default if you have more than one account set up on your iPad.

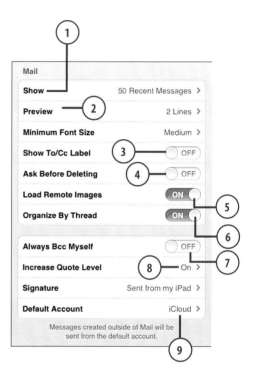

10. In most apps from which you send emails, you can type a message and also change the account you use to send the email.

New Message

From: ipadexample1@macmost.com

ipadexample1@macmost.c... ✓
ipadexample2@macmost.com
myipad2@macmost.com

(10)

Why Not Show Remote Images?

The main reason to not show remote images is bandwidth. If you get an email that has 15 images referenced in it, you need to download a lot of data, and it takes a while for that email to show up completely. However, remote images are often used as ways to indicate whether you have opened and looked at messages. So, turning this off might break some statistics and receipt functionality expected from the sender.

Setting Up Messaging

Even though your iPad isn't a phone, you can send text messages. The catch is that you can only message others who are also using Apple's iMessage system. This would include anyone using iOS 5 with an iPad, iPhone, or iPod touch, as long as they have signed up for the free service.

1. Launch the Messages app.

(1)

2. If this is your first time, you'll need to enter your Apple ID and password. Otherwise, you can go to step 3.

3. Tap Sign In.

iMessage

iMessages can be sent between iPhone, iPad, and iPod touch.
Learn more about iMessage ☉

Sign in with your Apple ID to activate iMessage.

(2)

Sign In **(3)**

Create New Account   >

4. You can use any valid email address that you own for Messages, even if it is not the same as your Apple ID email address. This will be the email address that others use to send you messages.

5. Tap Next.

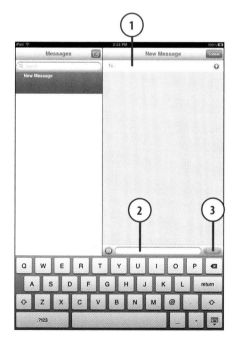

Conversing with Messages

After you have set up an account with Messages, you can quickly and easily send messages to others. The next time you launch Messages, you will be taken directly to the main screen.

1. In a new message, tap in the To field and enter the email address of the recipient. Note that they should already be signed up for iMessage or you will not be able to send them anything. Likewise, you can tap the + button to add a recipient from your contacts.

2. Tap the text field above the keyboard to type your message.

3. Tap Send to send your message.

4. You will see the conversation as a series of talk bubbles. Yours will appear on the right.

5. When your friend responds, you will see their talk bubbles as well.

6. A list of conversations appears on the left. You can have many going on at the same time, or use this list to look at old conversations.

7. You can send a picture as well as text by tapping the Picture button.

8. Tap the Compose button to start a new conversation.

9. Tap Edit to access buttons to delete old conversations.

10. Tap on the Person icon to do various tasks such as emailing the recipient, adding them to your contacts, or starting a FaceTime video chat.

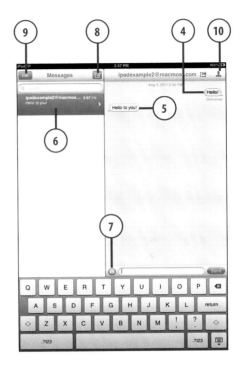

 ## Siri: Sending Email

You can use Siri to send email through a series of responses. First, activate Siri and say something like "Send an email to John." You will be asked for the subject of the message. After dictating that, you will be asked for the message text. Then, you will be shown the message to review it. You will then be asked "Ready to send it?" If you respond "yes," Siri will send the email. Otherwise, respond "no" to cancel.

Setting Up Twitter

Another way to message is to use the popular service Twitter. But instead of a private conversation, Twitter is all about telling the world what you are up to. If you already have a Twitter account, you can use the official Twitter app that comes with your iPad. Otherwise, you can set up a new account.

1. Install the Twitter app by going to Settings and tapping Twitter on the left side. Launch the Twitter app from the Home screen.

2. If you already have an account, tap Sign In.

3. If you need to create a Twitter account, you can do so here by tapping Sign Up. Then enter the required information for a new account.

4. Enter your Twitter Username and Password.

5. Tap Save.

Following People on Twitter

Even if you don't tweet much yourself, you can have fun with Twitter by following others. You can even learn things and stay informed. The key is to figure out who you want to follow and then add them.

1. Tap the Search button.

2. Type in the name or Twitter handle of the person you wish to follow.

3. Tap the People button.

4. Tap the profile that matches your search, and then use the picture to help identify the right person.

5. Tap the Follow button to add them to the list of people you follow.

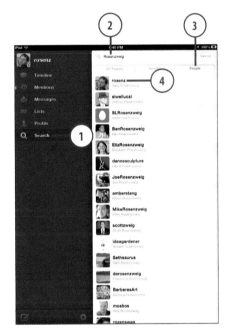

Who to Follow?

This depends on what you want from Twitter. If you just want to know what your friends are up to, then only follow your friends. If you want to hear what celebrities have to say, then search for some of your favorites. You can also search for professional and industry experts to learn more and stay informed. And don't limit your search to people. Local and worldwide news publications and organizations also have Twitter feeds.

How to Tweet

Thinking about adding your voice to the conversation? You can send a tweet easily with the Twitter app.

1. Tap the Compose button.

2. Enter the text of your tweet. It must be 140 characters or less.

3. This button makes it easy to add references to another Twitter member. You can also just type @ and their Twitter name.

4. This button makes it easy to add hash tags, which help identify subjects in messages. For instance, you might type #Rockies instead of just Rockies when you are talking about the baseball team.

5. You can add a photo or video to your tweet. This will upload the image to the service you have selected in your Twitter preferences and put a link to the file in the tweet.

6. You can add your GPS location to the tweet.

7. Tap Send.

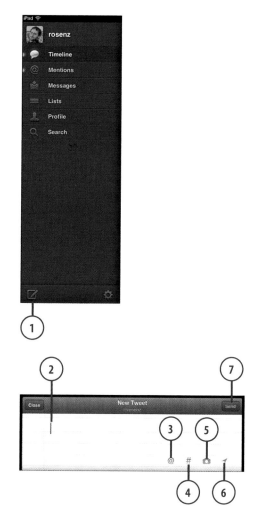

Siri: Tweeting

You can send a tweet with Siri simply by asking it to "send a tweet." You will then be prompted to speak the message. Like with sending email, you can review and confirm the message before it is sent.

Take pictures
with the iPad's
cameras.

Edit your photos
using iPhoto.

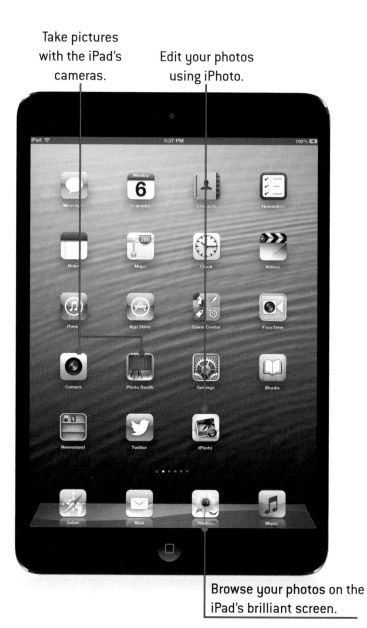

Browse your photos on the
iPad's brilliant screen.

In this chapter, we use the Camera app to take photos, the Photos app to view your pictures and create slideshows, and the iPhoto app to edit photos and create journals.

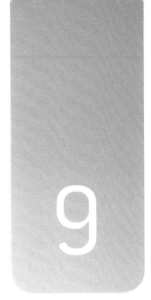

Taking and Editing Photos

In addition to replacing books, the iPad replaces photo albums. You can literally carry thousands of photos with you on your iPad. Plus, your iPad's screen is a beautiful way to display these photos.

To access photos on your iPad, you first must sync them from your computer. Then you can use the Photos app to browse and view your photos.

With the iPad's cameras, you can also take photos with your iPad. You can view those in the Photos app as well.

Taking Photos

The iPad mini includes two cameras that you can use to take photos. The primary app for doing this is the Camera app.

1. Launch the Camera app from the home page. This brings up the Camera app, and you should immediately see the image from the camera.

2. First, locate the switch at the bottom-right corner of the screen. Make sure it's switched to camera (left) instead of video (right).

3. Tap the button to the left of it to switch between front and rear cameras.

4. Tap anywhere on the image to specify that you want to use that portion of the image to determine the exposure for the photo.

5. After you have tapped on the image, and if you are using the rear-facing camera, you can zoom in. To do that, use your fingers to pinch apart. After you do so, you will see a zoom slider at the bottom of the screen.

6. Tap the Options button at the bottom of the screen to enable a transparent grid over image.

7. Tap the large camera button at the right side of the screen to take the picture.

8. Tap the button at the lower left to go to the Camera Roll and see the pictures you have taken.

9. Tap the middle of the image from the Camera Roll to bring up controls on the top and bottom of the screen.

10. Use the slider at the bottom to flip through images you have taken that are in your Camera Roll. Or just swipe left and right to flip through your photos.

11. Tap Camera Roll to exit viewing this one image and jump to an icon view of all of your Camera Roll photos.

12. Tap to start a slideshow of Camera Roll pictures.

13. Tap to email, print, or copy the photo. You can also send your photo via Twitter, Facebook, a text or email message, or to your iCloud Photo Stream.

14. Tap to send the photo to an Apple TV or other device using AirPlay.

15. Tap to delete the photo.

16. Tap Done to return to the Camera app to take another photo.

Using Photo Booth

In addition to the basic picture-taking functionality of the Camera app, you can also use the included Photo Booth app to take more creative shots using one of eight special filters.

1. Launch the Photo Booth app.

2. You'll start by seeing all the filters you can choose from. Tap one of the filters to select it.

3. Now you'll see just that one filter. In addition, you have some buttons. Tap on the button at the bottom right to switch between the front and rear cameras.

4. Tap the button at the bottom left to return to the 9-filter preview.

5. Tap the camera button at the bottom to take a picture.

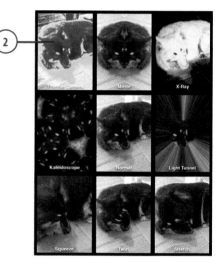

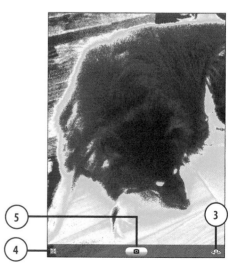

6. Some filters also allow you to tap the live video image to adjust the filter. For instance, the Light Tunnel filter enables you to set the position of the center of the tunnel.

7. As you take photos, they drop down to the bottom of the screen in a list. Select one and you'll get an X button to delete it.

8. Tap the button at the lower right to select photos to copy or email. All the pictures are placed in your Camera Roll as you take them, so you can also access them from the Photos app.

A Kind of Flash

When you take a picture with the camera on the front of the iPad, you get a kind of flash effect from the screen. It simply turns all white for a second. This helps in low light situations.

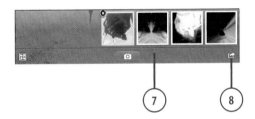

Browsing Your Photos

After you have synced to your Mac or PC, you should have some photos on your iPad, provided you have set some to sync in either iPhoto or iTunes. Then you can browse them with the Photos app.

1. Tap on the Photos app icon to launch it.

2. Tap one of the viewing options. You should have two to five choices, depending on how you synced your iPad.

3. Tap Photos to make sure you are in photo viewing mode.

4. Drag and scroll vertically or flick vertically to move through all the photos on your iPad.

5. Tap a photo to view that one. For most photos, you might want to rotate the iPad to its horizontal orientation for wide-screen viewing.

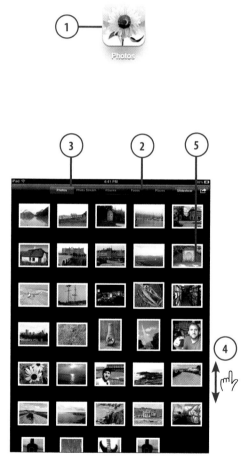

What Is Photo Stream?

Notice the Photo Stream select at the top of the screen? If you are using Apple's iCloud service, when you take pictures with an iOS device, they will show up in your Photo Stream. So taking a picture with an iPhone will put the picture in both the Photo Stream on your iPhone and on your iPad. They will also show up in iPhoto if you have a Mac. Apple TV also has the capability to show your Photo Stream. You don't have to do anything once iCloud has been configured on both; Photo Stream is just one of the many things that iCloud keeps in sync between devices.

6. To move to the next or previous photo, drag left or right.

7. To bring up controls at the top and bottom of a photo, tap in the center of the screen.

8. You can tap and run your finger over the small thumbnails at the bottom of the screen to move through photos.

9. Tap the All Photos button at the top of the screen to return to the list of photos.

ZOOM AND ROTATE

Here are a few tips on how to navigate your photos as you view them:

- Touch two fingers to the screen while viewing a photo, and pinch or unpinch to zoom out and in.

- Double-tap a photo to zoom back out to normal size.

- While a photo is at normal size, double-tap to zoom it to make it fit on the screen with the edges cropped.

- If you pinch in far enough, the picture closes, and you return to the browsing mode.

Editing Photos

You can edit the photos on your iPad by cropping them, rotating them, and enhancing the image quality.

1. Tap on the Photos app icon to launch it.

2. While viewing a photo, tap the Edit button to start editing.

3. Tapping the Rotate button rotates the image 90 degrees counterclockwise.

4. Tapping the Enhance button automatically adjusts the brightness, contrast, and other quality settings. There is no way to manually adjust the image; you simply tap this button and hope the result is something better than what you had before.

5. Tap the Red-Eye button to indicate the position of the eyes in the image and remove the red-eye effect that may have been caused by the flash.

6. Tap the Crop button to select a portion of the image. You can also slightly rotate the image to straighten it in this mode.

7. At any time, you can tap the Revert to Original button to remove all changes and start again.

8. After you have applied the first change, you can use the Undo button to undo the change. You can use it multiple times to undo a series of changes.

9. When you have made some changes and wish to save the image, tap the Save button. This creates a new copy of the image in your photo library with all the changes you have made.

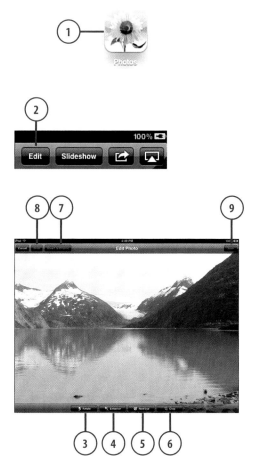

Sharing Photos

There are many ways you can share photos from the Photos app.

1. While viewing a single image in the Photos app, tap the boxed arrow button in the upper-right corner.

2. Tap Mail to send the current photo in an email message.

3. After you tap Mail, a message composition screen appears and starts a new message. The photo is attached to the message.

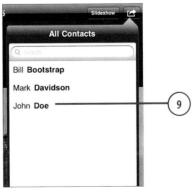

It's Not the Original Image

If you sync a photo from your computer to your iPad, and then email it to people, they actually receive a reduced image, not the original. iPad albums contain reduced images to save space. If you want to send the original, email it from your computer.

4. You can also send the photo to someone else using the iMessage system. See "Setting Up Messaging" in Chapter 8.

5. If you are using iCloud's Photo Stream feature, you can send the photo to Photo Stream—even if it is not a photo you have taken with the iPad's camera, such as a photo taken with your iPhone.

6. You can also send the photo to your Twitter account. Tap here and a small Twitter composition dialog will appear, which allows you to add a message to go along with the photo.

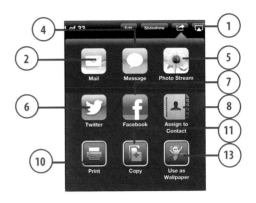

7. Likewise, you can also post the photo along with a message to your Facebook wall.

8. Tap Assign to Contact to display a list of all your contacts so that you can add the photo to the contact's thumbnail image.

9. Tap a contact name to assign the image to that contact.

10. Tap Print to send to your networked printer. See "Printing from Your iPad" in Chapter 18.

11. Tap Copy to copy the photo to your clipboard. Putting the photo on the clipboard enables you to paste it into documents or email messages in other apps.

12. To copy more than one image, tap the boxed arrow button while viewing your photos, and then select one or more photos to email or copy.

13. Tap Use as Wallpaper.

14. Assign the image to either the Lock Screen background or the Home Screen background, or both.

15. Tap the AirPlay button to show the photo on an Apple TV connected to the same network. This will only appear if you are using AirPlay on your network. Remember to have AirPlay turned on for that Apple TV.

You can share your photos in many ways, and it is likely that more will be added in the future. What you can use depends on what you have set up on your iPad. For instance, if you have Messaging and Twitter set up, you can use the Message and Tweet buttons to share using those services.

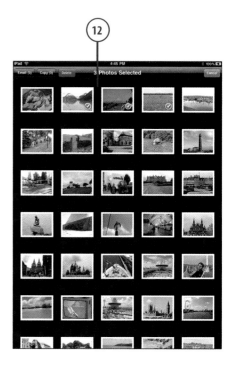

Viewing Albums

Looking at a huge list of photos is not the best way to view your collection. Using Albums is the simplest way to organize them.

1. In the Photos app, tap the Albums button. Most of the albums will correspond to your iPhoto albums or your folders if you sync images from your computer's file system.

2. Tap on an album to expand it to see all the photos.

3. Tap any photo to view it.

4. Tap the album name to return from viewing the photo, and then tap the Albums button on the next screen to return to the list of albums.

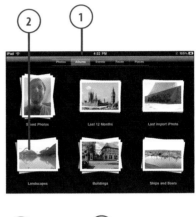

Getting Back to the Album

After you finish digging down into an album, you can go back to the list of albums by pressing the Albums button, or a similarly named button, at the top left. But you can also pinch in all photos to group them in the middle of the screen and then release to move back to the albums list.

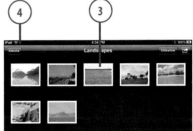

5. Tap Places to see your geo-tagged photos (those marked with GPS locations). You need to be using Places in iPhoto on your Mac for this to appear.

6. Tap a pin on the map and a set of photos appears above it.

7. Tap the set of photos to dig down into the pictures.

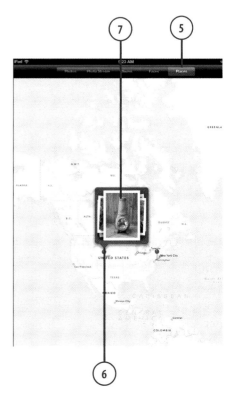

Creating Albums

You can create new albums right on your iPad. The process involves naming a new album and then selecting the photos to appear in the album.

1. Tap the Photos app icon to launch it.

2. Tap Albums at the top to view your albums.

3. Tap the Edit button to go into Editing mode.

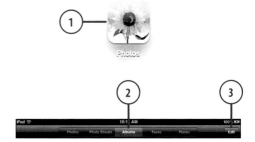

4. Tap New Album to start a new photo album.

5. You will be prompted to enter a name for the new album.

6. Tap the photos you want to appear in your new album. A checkmark appears on the ones you have selected.

7. You can use the Photo Stream, Albums, Faces, and Places buttons at the top of the screen to find photos.

8. Tap Done to complete the album.

You can edit any album you have created on your iPad, but not an album created on your computer and then synced to your iPad. Just go back to step 4, and select an iPad-created album instead of tapping the New Album button.

Creating a Slideshow

Another way to look at your photos is as a slideshow with music and transitions.

1. Tap on the Photos app icon to launch it.

2. Go to your Photos list, or select Albums, Event, Faces, or Places.

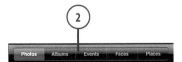

3. Tap the Slideshow button.

4. Switch the Play Music button on or off.

5. If you want to use music, tap to select a song from your iTunes collection.

6. Choose a transition.

7. Tap Start Slideshow.

Stopping a Slideshow

Tap on the screen anywhere to stop a slideshow.

Slideshow on TV

Want to present a slideshow on a monitor or TV? Use one of the video adapters discussed in Chapter 18 to hook your iPad up to a projector or a TV. Or, you can use AirPlay to stream the slideshow from your iPad to an Apple TV or other AirPlay device. Just tap on the slideshow while it is running and look for the AirPlay button at the upper-right corner. See "Using AirPlay to Play Music and Video on Other Devices" in Chapter 4.

Turning Your iPad into a Picture Frame

You can also set your iPad to show a slideshow when you are not in the Photos app. The Picture Frame function is configured in Settings, and then you activate it from the Lock screen.

1. Go to the Settings app.

2. Tap Picture Frame.

3. Choose either the Dissolve or Origami transition.

4. Turn Zoom in on Faces on or off. When it is on, pictures with faces in them are zoomed and cropped to show the faces close up.

5. Turn Shuffle on to show photos in random order.

6. Choose either All Photos, Albums, Faces, or Events.

7. Depending on your choice in step 6, you can check off one or more albums, faces, or events.

Picture Frame Album

If you want ultimate control over your picture frame slideshow and you use a Mac, create a special album in the Photos apps called something like "iPad Picture Frame" and fill it with just the photos you want to use. Make sure you set iTunes to sync this photo album. Then set your Picture Frame settings to show only this one album.

8. Lock your iPad by pressing the Wake/Sleep button at the top of the device.

9. Press the Home button to bring up the Lock screen.

10. Without unlocking your iPad, tap the Picture Frame button to the right of the Slide to Unlock switch to put your iPad in Picture Frame mode.

11. Tap the screen at any time to bring back the Lock Screen controls so that you can unlock your iPad.

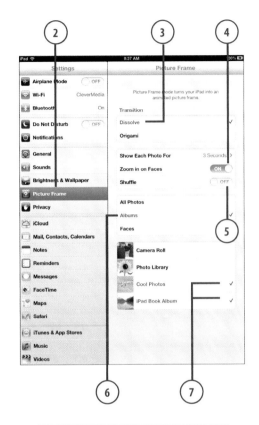

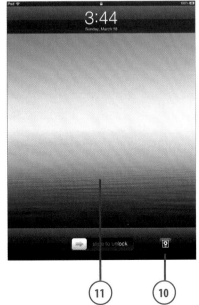

Capturing the Screen

You can capture the entire iPad screen and send it to your Photos app. This feature is useful if you want to save what you see to an image for later.

1. Make sure the screen shows what you want to capture. Try the Home screen, as an example.

2. Press and hold the Wake/Sleep button and Home button at the same time. The screen flashes and you hear a camera shutter sound, unless you have the volume turned down.

3. Go to the Photos app.

4. Tap on the Camera Roll album. The last image in this album should be your new screen capture. Tap it to open it.

5. The example is a vertical capture of the Home screen, so it might be confusing to look at. Turn your iPad horizontally.

6. Tap the boxed arrow icon to email the photo or copy it to use in another application. Or you can leave the photo in your Saved Photos album for future use.

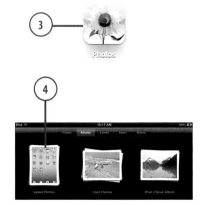

Deleting Photos

You can only delete photos from the Camera Roll album (sometimes referred to as the "Saved Photos" album) and your Photo Stream.

1. In Photos, go to the Albums view.

2. Tap on Camera Roll.

3. Tap a photo to view it.

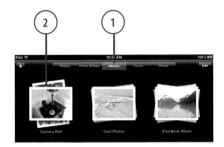

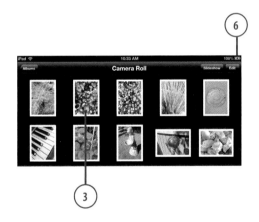

4. Tap the Trash Can button.

5. Tap Delete Photo.

6. Alternatively, you can go back to step 2 and then tap the boxed arrow button.

7. Tap multiple photos to select them.

8. Tap Delete, and then tap Delete Selected Photos.

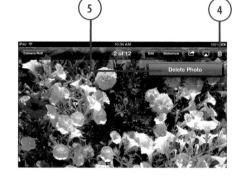

So How Can I Delete Other Photos?

The Camera Roll album is special; it contains photos created on your iPad. The rest of the albums are just copies of photos synced from your computer. You can't delete them from your iPad any more than you can delete music synced to your iPad.

To delete these photos, go back to iPhoto on your computer, and remove them from any albums that you have set to sync to your iPad. Also, go into iTunes on your computer, and make sure the photo syncing options there—such as to sync Last 12 Months—won't copy that photo.

If you think of your photos like you think of your music, understanding which photos are synced and why makes more sense.

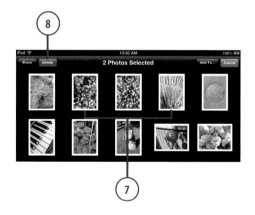

Adjusting Photos in iPhoto

Although the Photos app gives you the ability to make basic adjustments to your pictures, the iPhoto app goes much further. You need to purchase it in the App Store. Then you can use the iPhoto app to apply a variety of filters, adjustments, and special effects to your photos.

1. After you purchase and download iPhoto, tap its icon to run it.

2. First, you need to select a photo to edit. Tap Albums to view your photos grouped into the same albums as in the Photos app.

3. You can view the photos you have taken with your iPad's camera in the Camera Roll. You can also see photos you have created in other apps here.

4. If you have already edited a photo, you will see the Edited album. This contains a list of all altered photos. You can go here to continue to work on them.

5. Tap Photos to see one long list of all the photos on your iPad.

6. Tap an album to dig into that album's photos.

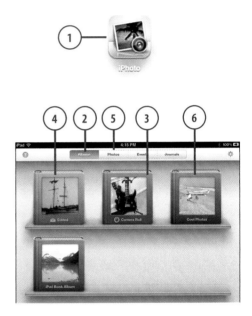

7. You will see one of the photos from the album in the center of the screen. This is the photo you are currently editing.

8. Tap the Thumbnail Grid button to see the rest of the photos in the album at the bottom so that you can switch between them.

9. Tap any photo to switch to it. Alternatively, you can swipe left or right to move between photos.

10. Tap the Edit button to bring up the photo editing controls at the bottom of the screen.

11. Tap the Help button to bring up labels for all of buttons and controls in iPhoto.

12. Try the Auto-enhance button if you want to let your iPad figure out how to adjust the brightness, contrast, and other alterations that should improve the look of the picture.

13. Tap the Exposure button to reveal the brightness and contrast controls.

14. Drag the brightness control left or right to adjust the general brightness of the photo.

15. Drag the contrast controls left or right to adjust the contrast.

16. Drag the shadows control to adjust the exposure for the dark areas of the photo.

17. Drag the highlights control to adjust the exposure for the light areas of the photo.

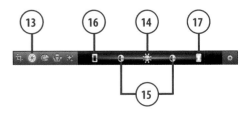

18. Tap the Color adjustments button.

19. Drag the Saturation control left and right to saturate or desaturate the image. The first enhances the color in your photo, and the second removes color, bringing it closer to black and white.

20. Adjust the blue tones in the picture.

21. Adjust the green tones in the picture.

22. Adjust the skin tones in the picture.

23. Bring up a set of white balance controls.

Cropping, Straightening, and Rotating

In addition to color effects and adjustments, you can also crop and rotate your pictures. The Crop & Straighten button is at the bottom-left corner and enables you to trim the edges down and rotate the image any amount. In addition, the Rotate 90 degrees button along the bottom of the screen (an arrow next to a rectangle) lets you quickly rotate an image that is oriented incorrectly.

Using Brushed Effects on Photos in iPhoto

There are also adjustments that you can make on parts of a photo rather than the entire image.

1. Tap the Brushes button.

2. Select a brush to use.

3. Use your finger to manually brush the area you want the effect applied to. For instance, you can desaturate everything in this photo except the fire.

4. Tap the undo button to revert to how the image was before you tried the brush. Using the undo button, you can try a variety of brushes and other effects knowing that you can undo the change easily.

5. Tap the Show Original button if you want to quickly compare your changes to the original photo without undoing the changes.

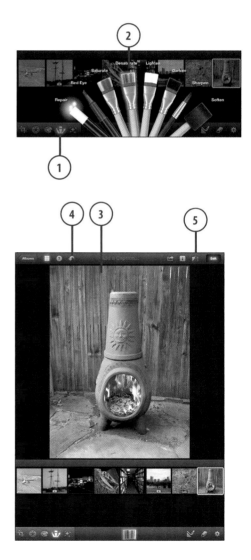

Applying Special Effects to Photos in iPhoto

You can also apply a variety of filters to your entire photo.

1. Tap the Effects button.

2. Select one of the effects sets.

3. Tap a thumbnail to try that effect.

4. Use undo to revert back to the original image before trying another one.

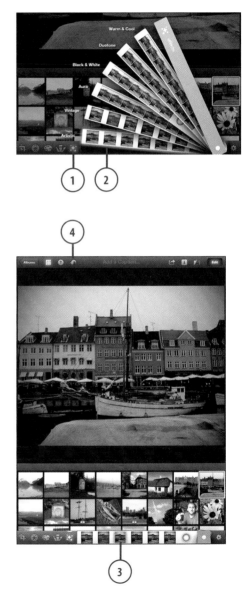

Sharing Photos with iPhoto

Whether you edit the photo or not, you can still use iPhoto to share your photos in a variety of ways with different services and devices.

1. Tap the Share button to bring up the list of sharing methods.

2. Tap Camera Roll to send the photo to your iPad's Camera Roll as a new image. Use this to allow other apps to access your edited photo and to send the photo to your computer the next time you sync your photos.

3. Tap iTunes to prepare the image to be shared with your computer via iTunes sync. See "Syncing Documents" in Chapter 3.

4. Tap Email to compose a message with the selected pictures.

5. Tap Beam to send the picture wirelessly to another iOS device.

6. When you select Beam, or almost any other sharing option, the next step is to select which images to send.

7. When you Beam an image, you need to select the iOS device to send it to. The other device needs to be on the same Wi-Fi network and running the same iPhoto iOS app.

8. You can send a photo to an AirPrint printer. See "Printing from Your iPad" in Chapter 18.

9. You can post a photo online and send a tweet with a link to it.

10. You can add the photo to your Flickr account.

11. You can also post a photo to Facebook.

12. You can start a slideshow with photos you select.

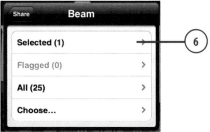

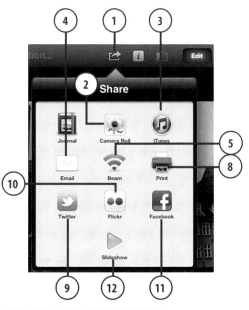

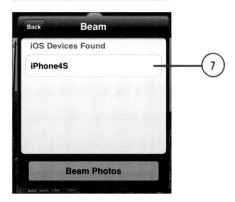

Creating Online Journals with iPhoto

You can also post photos online using Apple's free iCloud service. The Journals feature of iPhoto allows you to create web pages with one or more photos on them, plus additional information like text and maps.

To begin, it is best to select several photos. Then share and use the Journals function.

1. Tap the special tools button.

2. Tap Select Multiple.

3. Select several photos.

4. Tap Done.

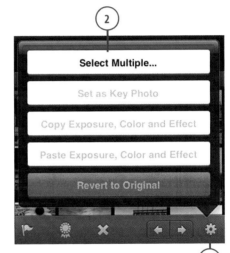

5. The selected photos now appear in the middle of the screen.

6. Tap the Share button

7. Tap Journal.

8. Tap Selected.

9. Enter a name for your new journal.

10. Swipe through the themes and select one.

11. Tap Create Journal.

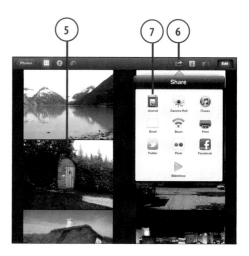

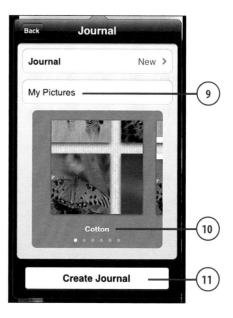

12. Tap Show.

13. Photos are automatically placed on the page.

14. Tap Edit to move or resize photos and to add more content to the page.

15. You can drag a picture to move it by tapping and holding on the photo for a second, and then moving it around after it "detaches" from the page. You can also drag the blue dots around it to resize it. Other pictures automatically reflow to fit.

16. You can also remove a picture.

17. You can edit a picture using iPhoto's effects and filters.

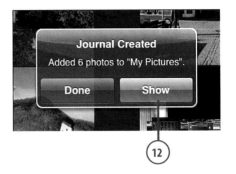

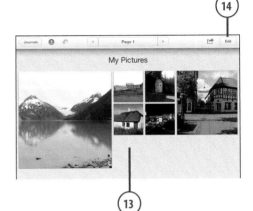

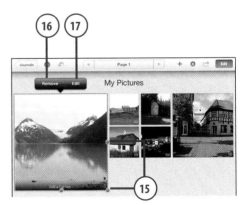

18. Tap the + button.

19. You can add text to your page in a variety of formats, such as a sticky note or torn strip of paper. Text objects can be resized and moved like pictures.

20. You can add a map to your page.

21. You can add a graphic with the date on it.

22. You can add a weather graphic.

23. Tap the Page button to create a second page. Journals can have just one, or many, pages.

24. Tap the Edit button to leave Edit mode. Only then will the Share button become active.

25. Tap Share.

26. You can send the Journal to your iCloud account. This will create one or more web pages. You can then send your friends links to those pages and they can view your journal.

27. You can also save the files that make up the journal web pages. You would then transfer them to your Mac or PC using iTunes. See "Syncing Documents" in Chapter 3. This is for anyone with their own website who knows how to upload and manipulate files on the server.

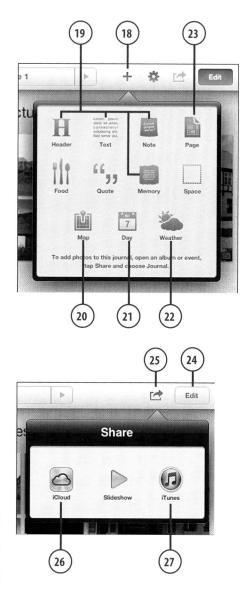

That's a basic overview of Journals to get you started. It is a very deep, creative tool. After you create your first journal, you will see a new album appear in iPhoto with your journals. You can go back to one you have created and edit it at any time. Sharing it again to iCloud will update that journal.

To make the most of the Journals feature of iPhoto, you will want to explore it on your own. Use some of your favorite photos and try different sizes and positions for each. Try adding each of the special elements like maps and notes. Once you get to know this tool, you will be able to quickly create fun and interesting web pages to show off your photos to friends.

Record video with your iPad's two cameras.

Make video calls with FaceTime.

Put together movies from your video clips and photos.

In this chapter, we use the Camera, Photo Booth, and iMovie apps to shoot and edit video with your iPad. We'll also use the FaceTime app to make a video call.

Recording Video

You can record video using either of the two cameras on your iPad. The primary app for doing this is the Camera app.

In addition, you can edit video with the iMovie app. This app, which you can purchase from Apple in the App Store, lets you combine clips and add transitions, titles, and audio.

The cameras on your iPad can also be used to video chat with someone on another iPad, an iPhone, iPod Touch, or a Mac using the FaceTime app.

Shooting Video

If you simply want to record something that is happening using the cameras, you can do it with the Camera app.

1. Launch the Camera app.

2. Switch the camera mode to video.

3. Toggle between the rear and front cameras.

4. Optionally, tap in the image to set the best point for the exposure setting.

5. Start recording. While you are recording, the red dot will flash and the length of the recording will show in the upper-right corner. Tap the same button to stop recording.

6. Tap the image in the lower-left corner to view your video when you are done.

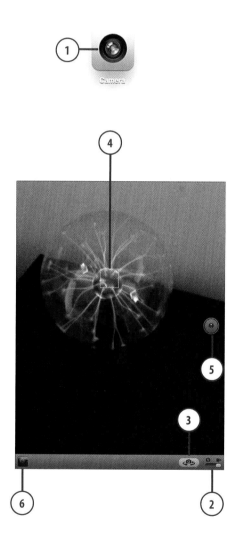

7. You are now in the Camera Roll, the same place as you were in "Taking Photos," in Chapter 9. But the interface looks different when you have a video instead of a still photo. Tap the play button to watch the video.

8. Tap the boxed arrow button to email the video, or send it to your YouTube account or via a text message.

9. Tap the AirPlay button to stream the video over Apple TV or another AirPlay device.

10. Tap the trashcan to delete the video.

11. When you are done viewing your video, tap Done to shoot another.

It's Not All Good

EMAILING COMPRESSES THE VIDEO

Video with the rear camera is shot at 1920x1080. But when you email a video, it's compressed to a much smaller size—536x320 in the case of the 3rd generation iPad. This is good because you won't be sending a massive video file, using your bandwidth and the bandwidth of the recipient. But don't use email to save your videos to your computer. Instead, sync and transfer, as you would do with photos.

Trimming Video Clips

While viewing a video in the Camera Roll, you can also trim it to cut some unneeded footage from the start and end of the video.

1. You can get to the Camera Roll by either using the Photos app or the Camera app. For instance, launch the Camera app and immediately tap the image in the lower left on the screen.

2. If you are viewing a video, you will see a timeline of sorts at the top of the screen.

3. Drag the left side of the timeline to the left to trim from the start of the video.

4. Drag the right side of the timeline to the right to trim from the end of the video.

5. Tap the Trim button.

6. Tap Trim Original to replace the video with the trimmed version.

7. Tap Save as New Clip to keep the original, and also save your trimmed version as a separate clip.

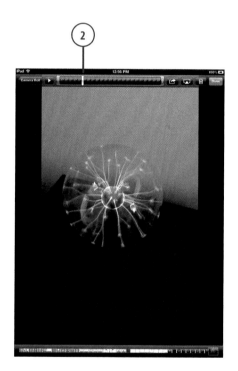

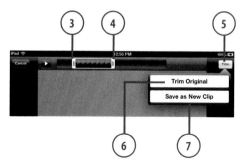

Combining Clips in iMovie

The trimming functionality of the Camera and Photos apps gives you the basic ability to edit a video clip, but you can go a lot further if you purchase the iMovie app from Apple. Although not a full-featured editor like you might have on your computer, you can combine clips, add titles and transitions, and produce a short video from your clips.

1. Launch the iMovie app. Turn your iPad to look at the screen horizontally. iMovie is a little easier to use in that orientation.

2. Tap the + button, and then New Project, to create a new project.

3. You can add a video to your project by tapping on a clip on the left, and then tapping the blue down arrow to place it in the timeline at the bottom.

4. You can also record new video clips using the camera button at the right.

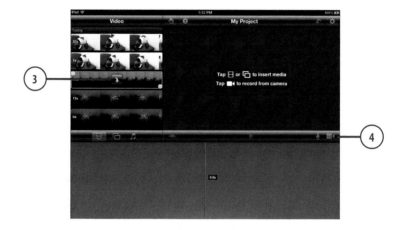

5. Continue to add more clips. Each one will be appended to the end of the project.

6. The red line indicates the current position of the video.

7. The preview area shows you the image at the current position.

8. You can drag the project timeline left and right to scroll through it.

9. You can pinch in and out to shrink or enlarge the timeline.

10. Press play to play the video in the preview area. If the red line is at the end of the video, it will jump back to the start of the video first.

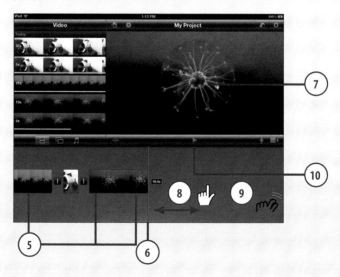

11. Tap and hold a clip, and you can drag it to a different part of the project timeline.

12. Tap the My Projects button when you are done editing. There is no need to "save" your project—the current state of the project is always saved.

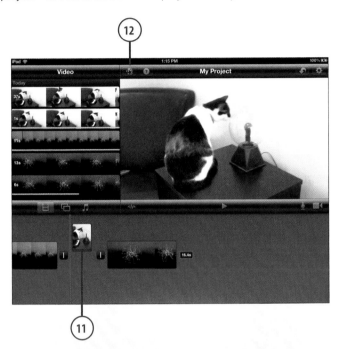

13. Tap the name of the project in the theater marquee to edit the name.

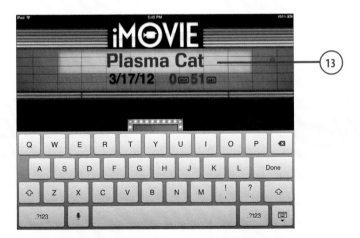

14. Tap the play button to view the finished project.

15. Tap the export button to send the video to your Camera Roll, export it to iTunes the next time you sync, or upload to one of the listed Internet video sites.

Best Way to Share with Friends?

While it may seem to be a good idea to simply email a video to your friends, remember that video files are usually very large. Even if you have the bandwidth to upload them, your friends need the bandwidth to download them. Some may have restrictions on how large email attachments can be.

So, the video sharing options in iMovie are better for all concerned. You can upload to your Facebook or YouTube account and even set the video to "private" or "unlisted." Then just let a few friends know about it with the link in an email instead of a huge file attachment.

Editing Transitions in iMovie

Between each clip in your iMovie project is a transition. You can choose between a direct cut (no transition), a cross-dissolve transition, or a special theme transition. But first, you must select a theme.

1. Open up the project you created in the previous example.

2. Tap the settings button at the upper right to select a theme.

3. Flip through the themes and choose one.

4. Double-tap one of the transition buttons that appear between each clip. This should bring up the Transition Settings menu.

5. Choose None if you want one clip to start right after the other.

6. Choose Cross Dissolve if you want one clip to fade into the other.

7. Choose Theme to use the special theme transition. These vary depending on which theme you choose.

8. Choose a duration for the transition.

9. Tap the triangles below the transition button to expand into a precision editor.

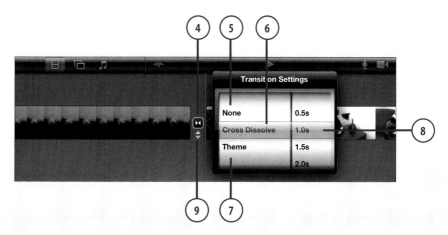

10. Move the transition area to select how you want the two clips to overlap during the transition.

11. Tap the triangles to leave the precision edit mode.

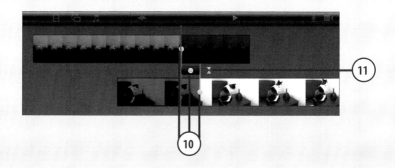

Transition Previews?

Unfortunately, you can't really preview the transitions in iMovie for iPad. You just have to apply a theme and then see what the transitions look like. Plus, the theme applies to the entire project, so you can't mix and match transitions. iMovie for iPad doesn't give you much control over the details. It is more for people who want to create a quick, nice-looking video without playing around with the details.

Adding Photos to Your Video in iMovie

You can also add photos from your Camera Roll or any album on your iPad. You can just use a series of photos in a video, or mix photos and video clips.

1. Continuing with the previous example, scroll the timeline all the way to the left.

2. Tap the photos button.

3. Tap the name of the album that contains your photo.

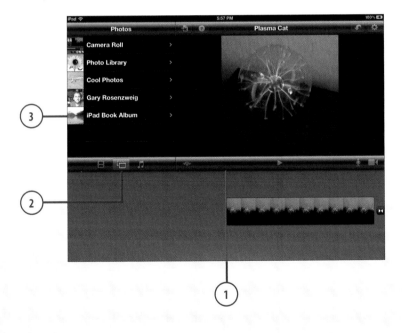

4. Tap the photo you want to use.

5. It now appears in the timeline at the current position. Tap it to select it.

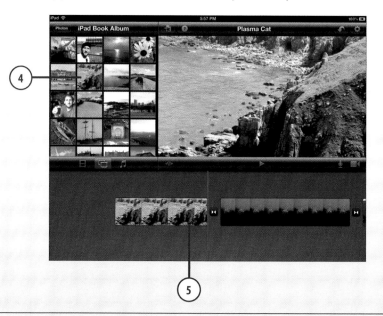

Pictures in Projects

Pictures in iMovie projects don't just sit there; they move. For instance, the picture may start out fitting in the screen, and then slowly zoom in on a specific spot. Or, it may start showing the upper left and pan down to the lower right. You can control where the movement starts and ends.

GETTING CREATIVE WITH PICTURES

You can even create a video without any photos. For example, you could use one of the drawing programs mentioned in Chapter 16, such as SketchBook Pro, Brushes, ArtStudio, or Adobe Ideas, to create images with text and drawings on them. Create a series to illustrate an idea or story. Then bring them together as a series of pictures in an iMovie project. Add music and a voice over to make something very interesting.

6. Tap and drag the yellow dots to change the duration of the photo in the timeline. It starts with a default of 5 seconds. But, for example, you could increase it to 10 seconds.

7. Tap the Start button that appears in the preview area. Then adjust the photo by pinching zooming and dragging to get it just as you like. For instance, pinch in so the photo fits into the frame.

8. Tap the End button at the upper right to set the end position for the picture. For instance, unpinch to zoom in on a specific area.

9. Tap Done when you finish adjusting both the start and end positions.

10. Slide the timeline back and forth to preview how the movement in the picture will work.

You can continue to add pictures just as you would add video clips. Add as many as you like. You can even create a slideshow of just photos without ever shooting a single second of video footage.

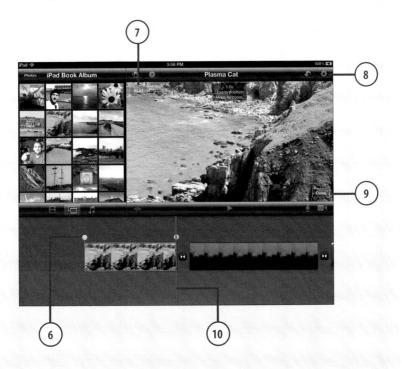

Adding Video Titles in iMovie

You can also add titles that overlay clips or photos in iMovie. Like the transitions, the style of the titles depends on the theme you are using.

1. Continue with the example we have been building. Double-tap on a clip to select it and bring up the Clip Settings menu.

2. Tap Title Style.

3. Select a title style. As you do so, a preview appears in the preview area.

4. Tap in the text field area in the preview to bring up the keyboard, and enter text.

5. Some title types show a map or have a space where the location is displayed. Tap Location to enter a name for the location.

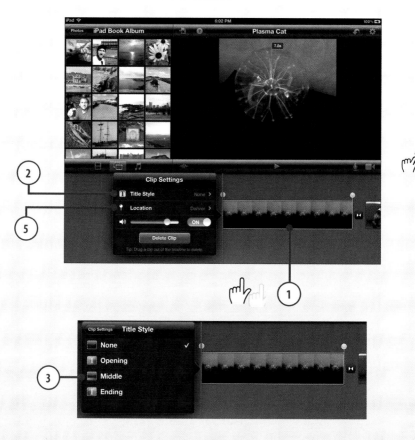

MUSIC AND VOICEOVERS

You can also do a lot with the audio in iMovie. You can add any song from your iPad's iTunes collection to the video as the background track. There are also a number of theme music tracks included that you can use.

You can also add from a collection of sound effects the same way. However, sound effects can appear at any point in your movie, whereas music covers the entire span of the video.

You can also record a voiceover so you can narrate your video. This means you can have four audio tracks: the audio attached to the video, background music, sound effects, and a voiceover.

To learn how to use all the additional features of iMovie, look for the help button at the bottom-left corner of the projects screen. This brings up complete documentation for the app.

Setting Up FaceTime

Another major use of the video cameras is FaceTime. This is Apple's video call-ing service. You can make video phone calls between any devices that have FaceTime, including recent iPhones, iPod touches, iPads, and Macs. As the number of people with FaceTime increases, this app will become more useful.

All that's required to make a FaceTime call is a free account. You can use your existing Apple ID or create a new one. You can also assign alternate email addresses to be used as FaceTime "phone numbers" that people can use to contact you via FaceTime.

1. Launch the Settings app.

2. Tap FaceTime on the left.

3. Turn on FaceTime if it isn't already.

4. An Apple ID is needed for FaceTime even if you don't plan to use that same email address with FaceTime calls. If you haven't used FaceTime before, you will be prompted to enter your Apple ID and password.

5. This list contains email addresses others can use to reach you via a FaceTime call. By default, your Apple ID email address will be here. But you can add another one and even remove your Apple ID email address if you never want to use that for FaceTime.

6. The Caller ID represents your default email address used to place FaceTime calls. It is what others will see when you call them.

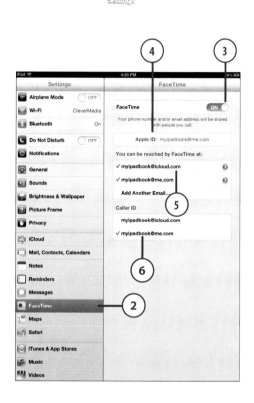

By using different email addresses for different iOS devices, you can more easily specify which device you are calling. For instance, if you and your spouse both have iPhones, and you share an iPad, you can give the iPad a different email address (maybe a free email account). That way you can specify which device you want to call.

Remember that you still need to be connected to the Internet with a Wi-Fi connection. At this time, mobile carriers do not support FaceTime over their 3G or 4G networks, although there are rumors they might in the near future, possibly for an extra charge.

Placing Video Calls with FaceTime

After you have your account set up in FaceTime, you can place and receive calls.

1. Launch the FaceTime app.

2. Select a contact from your list. If your contact list isn't showing, tap the Contacts button at the bottom right of the screen.

3. Alternatively, you can add a new contact. You need to know either their iPhone 4 phone number or the email address they used when creating their FaceTime account.

4. Tap the phone number or email address for the contact to initiate a FaceTime call.

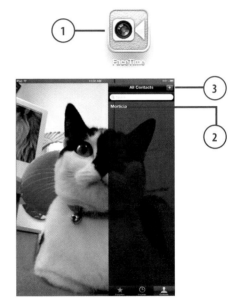

5. Wait while the call is placed. You'll hear a ringing. You can tap the End button to cancel the call.

6. After the other party has answered the call, you can see both her image filling the whole screen and your image in the upper right. You can drag your image to any of the four corners.

7. Tap the mute button to mute your microphone.

8. Tap the switch cameras button to show the view from the rear camera.

9. Tap End to finish the call.

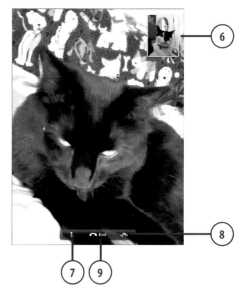

Two-Way Street

In order for you to place a FaceTime call, of course, the recipient also needs to have FaceTime set up. You can tell in step 4 that this has been done because of the blue camera icon next to the phone number. Otherwise, if she has a FaceTime-compatible device, you need to get her to set up an account before trying to initiate a FaceTime connection.

Receiving Video Calls with FaceTime

After you have a FaceTime account, you can receive calls as well. Make sure you have set up FaceTime by following the steps in the "Setting Up FaceTime" task earlier in this chapter. Then it is a matter of just waiting to receive a call from a friend.

1. If you aren't currently using your iPad, it will ring using the ringtone you choose in Settings, General, Sounds. When you pick up your iPad, you'll see something similar to the lock screen, but with a live feed from your camera (so you can see if you look good enough to video chat) and the caller's name at the top.

2. Slide the Slide to Answer button to the right to wake up your iPad and go immediately into the call. If you are using your iPad at the time the call comes in, FaceTime launches and you get a screen with two buttons. The screen will still show your camera's image and the name of the caller.

3. After the conversation starts, you can mute your microphone.

4. You can switch to the rear camera.

5. Tap End to end the call.

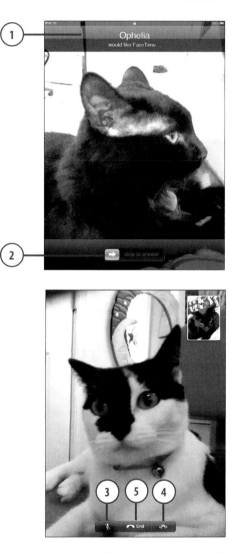

Ring Ring

Remember that you can set your ringtone in the Settings app under Sounds. You can even set the volume for rings to be unaffected by the volume controls on the side of your iPad. That way you don't miss a call because you left the volume turned down.

SO WHAT IF IT DOESN'T WORK?

FaceTime is set up to be simple. It just works. Except when it doesn't. There are no network settings to fiddle with. So the problem usually lies in the Wi-Fi router at either end of the call. If someone has security on their modem or Wi-Fi router, then it could be interfering with the call. See this document at Apple's site for some FaceTime troubleshooting tips:

http://support.apple.com/kb/ht4319.

Write and design
complex
documents.

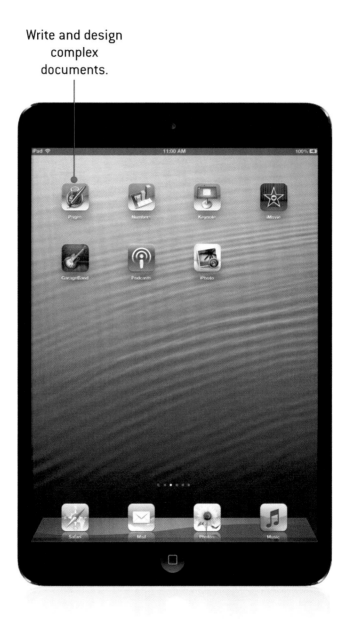

In this chapter, we begin to get work done on the iPad by using Pages to create and format documents.

→ Creating a New Document

→ Styling Text

→ Reusing Styles

→ Formatting Text

→ Creating Lists

→ Column Layouts

→ Inserting Images

→ Using Shapes in Documents

→ Creating Tables

→ Creating Charts

→ Document Setup

→ Sharing and Printing Documents

Writing with Pages

So far, we've mostly been looking at ways to consume media—music, video, books, photos, and so on. The next three chapters deal with the iWork suite of applications: Pages, Numbers, and Keynote.

We start with Pages, the word processor, which you can use for a fair amount of layout and design. Pages is not one of the iPad's built-in apps. You need to purchase and download it from the App Store.

Creating a New Document

Let's start off simple. The most basic use of Pages is to create a new document and enter some text.

1. Tap the Pages app icon on the Home screen.

2. If this is the first time you have run Pages, you will go through a series of screens welcoming you to Pages and asking if you want to set up iCloud as the storage space for Pages documents. Finally, it will ask if you want to create a new document or learn more about using Pages.

iCloud for iWork

Pages, Numbers, and Keynote can store their files on Apple's iCloud service rather than on your iPad. This is the default behavior as long as you have iCloud configured on your iPad and have allowed these three apps to use it. Using just an iPad means you won't notice much of a difference. You can take comfort, however, in knowing that they are being backed up on Apple servers as you work. And if you have a second iCloud device, like an iPhone or a Mac, you will see these documents there as well. For instance, Pages documents saved to iCloud from Pages on your iPad will appear in Pages for Mac. You can also access them at the iCloud website. See "Syncing Using iCloud" in Chapter 3.

3. If this isn't the first time you have run Pages, tap the + button at the top-left corner of the screen to start a new document.

4. Tap Create Document.

5. The template choices display. You can scroll vertically to see more. Tap the Blank template to go into the main editing view.

6. Type some sample text in the document just to get the feel for entering text.

7. Return to your documents list by tapping Documents.

8. You can now see all your documents. If you have not created any other documents yet, you should have two documents now: the one you just created and the sample document.

9. Tap a document to open it.

10. Tap Edit to select and then delete documents.

A Real Keyboard

If you plan on using Pages on your iPad often, you might want to invest in a physical keyboard for your iPad. You can use the Apple Wireless keyboard or almost any Bluetooth keyboard. Apple also has a version of the iPad dock that includes a keyboard. See Chapter 18, "iPad Accessories," for details.

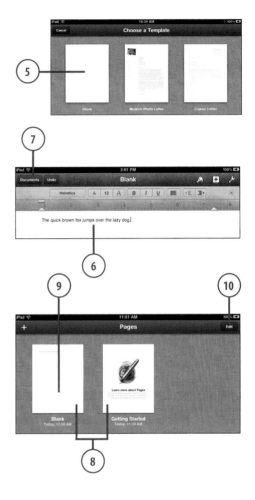

Styling Text

Now let's learn how to style text. You can change the font, style, and size.

1. In an open document, double-tap a word to select it.

2. Pull on the blue dots to select the area you want to style.

3. Use the toolbar buttons to format your text as bold, italic, or underline.

Undo Mistakes

At the top of the Pages screen, there is an Undo button. Use that to undo the last action you took—whether it is typing some text or changing styles. You can use Undo multiple times to go back several steps.

4. Tap the paintbrush button to bring up the Style/List/Layout menu.

5. Tap Style.

6. Tap the B, I, and U buttons to format text. Tap the buttons a second time if you want to change the style back to plain text. The fourth button, S, styles the text as strikethrough.

7. Tap the size and name of the font.

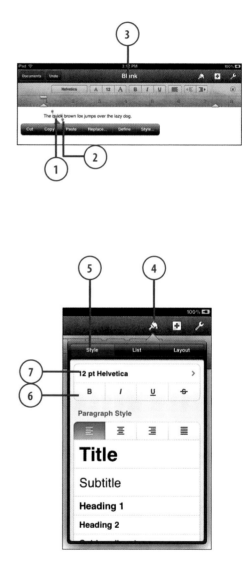

8. Set the font size, color, and type. Tap on the top and bottom halves of the font size indicator to increase and decrease the font size.

9. Tap the Color button to get a selection of colors.

10. Tap a color or swipe to the left to look at the page containing gray-scale options.

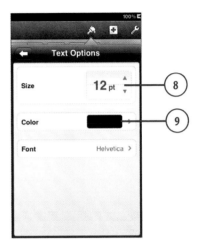

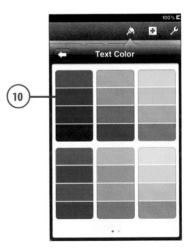

11. The black color tile has a check mark in it to indicate that it is the current color of the text. Swipe right to get back to the first page of colors and choose a different color, such as red.

12. Tap the left-facing arrow above the colors to return to the Text Options menu.

13. Tap Font.

14. Drag up and down in the list of fonts to view them all.

15. Tap a font to change the selected text to it.

16. Tap the blue button if it appears to the right of a font to view variations for that font.

17. Tap outside of the menu to dismiss it and return to editing.

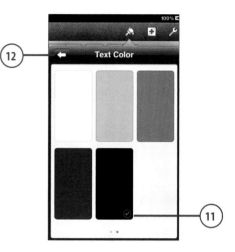

Printing Pages

You can print a document from Pages, Numbers, or Keynote if you have one of the printers compatible with Apple's AirPrint technology built into your iPad. Tap the tool button (it looks like a wrench in the upper-right corner) and then tap Print. You'll be prompted to select a printer, page range, and number of copies. See "Printing from Your iPad" in Chapter 18.

Paragraph Styles

There are many preset styles that apply to an entire paragraph, such as Title, Subtitle, Heading 1, Body, and so on. Select one of these to apply that preset style to the entire paragraph, not just the selected text.

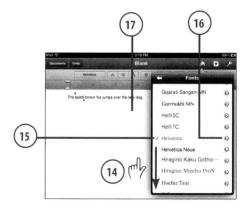

Reusing Styles

So, what if you define the font, style, and size for something in Pages, and you want to use it again with another section of text? Just copy and paste the style from one piece of text to others.

1. Select some text.

2. Tap Style.

3. Tap Copy Style.

4. Select a piece of text to which you want to paste that style.

5. Repeat steps 2 and 3 to show the Copy Style and Paste Style button, and then tap Paste Style.

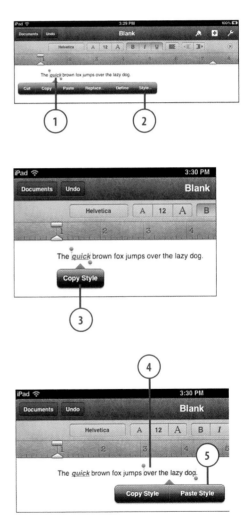

Formatting Text

The next step is to learn how to format and align text, which you do mostly through the toolbars at the top of the Pages screen in vertical mode.

1. Continue to work with the sample document, or start a new one and add some text.

2. Tap in the text so that the cursor is somewhere in the paragraph you want to format.

3. Tap the alignment button at the top.

4. Tap the center alignment button in the menu. You can use the left, right, or justified buttons in the same set to align the text differently.

5. Tap at the end of the line to place the cursor there.

6. Tap the return key on the onscreen keyboard to go to the next line.

7. Type some sample text, just a word or two.

8. Tap the alignment button again.

9. Tap Align Left in the drop-down menu.

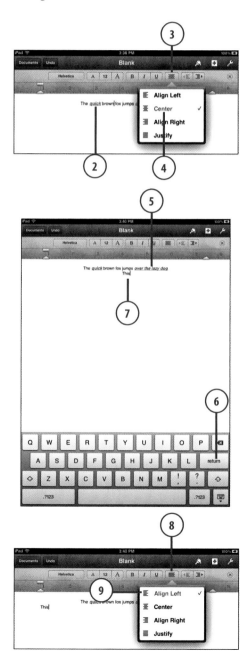

10. Double-tap next to the end of your text to bring up the Select, Select All, and Paste buttons.

11. Tap Insert to choose the element to insert.

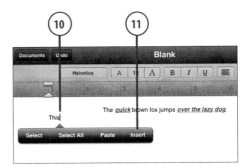

12. Tap Tab to insert a tab.

13. Type another sample word. Because the new line of text inherited the underline format of the previous line, we can clearly see the extra space inserted between the words by the tab. We haven't added any tab stops to the document yet, so the position just defaults to the next inch.

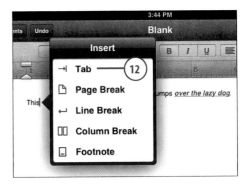

14. Tap in the ruler around the 2-inch marker to insert a tab stop, which moves the second word over to match this tab stop's horizontal position. You can tap and drag existing tab stops to reposition them.

More Tab Options

If you like tabs, you'll be happy to know you can make centered tabs, right tabs, and dotted tabs as you would on a desktop word processor. Just double-tap a tab in the ruler, and it changes to the next type. To remove a tab, just tap and drag it down and out of the ruler.

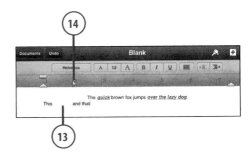

Creating Lists

You can easily create lists in Pages, just like in a normal word processor.

1. Create a new document in Pages using the Blank template.

2. Type a word that could be the first item in a list. Don't tap return.

3. Tap the paintbrush button on the toolbar.

4. Tap List.

5. Tap the Bullet option to turn the text you just typed into the first item in a bulleted list.

6. Use the on-screen keyboard to tap return and type several more lines. Tapping return always creates a new line in the list. Tapping return a second time ends the list formatting.

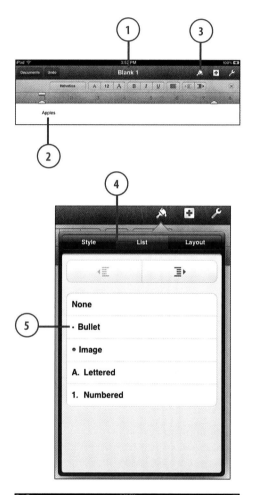

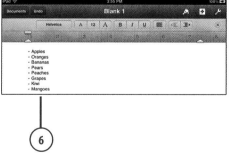

7. Select the entire list.

8. Tap the paintbrush button.

9. Tap Numbered to change the list to a numbered list.

10. Tap one line of the list.

11. Tap paintbrush again.

12. Tap the right arrow in the List menu to indent the line and create a sublist. You can create sublists as you type or by selecting lines and using the arrow buttons to format after you type.

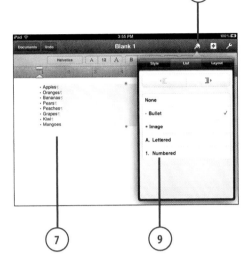

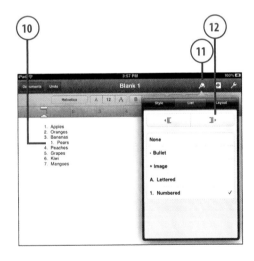

Column Layouts

Pages lets you go beyond boring one-column layouts. You can even change the number of columns for each paragraph.

1. Start a new document and fill it with text—perhaps copy and paste text from a website article. If you open a document, tap inside it so you are editing the document and you can see the keyboard at the bottom.

2. Tap the paintbrush button.

3. Tap Layout.

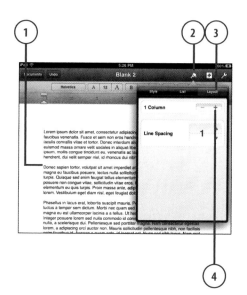

Line Spacing

The Layout menu includes duplicates of the alignment buttons and a Line Spacing setting. You can change the line spacing in one-quarter line increments. A change affects the text in the paragraph where the cursor is located or the text in all selected paragraphs.

4. Tap + next to Columns. This adds a column and the entire document changes to a 2-column layout. Continue tapping the + button to add more columns.

5. Tap – to reduce the number of columns until you are back to a 1-column layout.

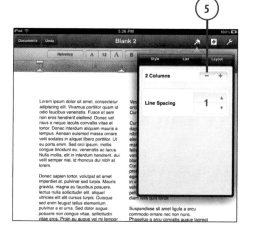

Using Different Column Formats

You can select just one paragraph and apply a two-column layout to it while leaving the rest of your document in one-column layout. Be aware, though, that switching between one column and multiple columns in the same document can yield unpredictable results, so proceed with caution.

Inserting Images

You can place images into your Pages documents. You can even wrap text around the images.

1. Open a new document and fill it with text.

2. Place the cursor somewhere in the text, such as at the beginning of the second paragraph.

3. Tap the + button.

4. Tap Media.

5. Select a photo from a photo album.

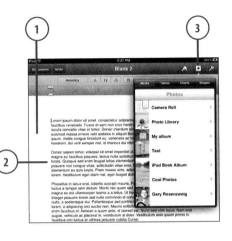

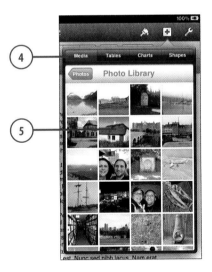

6. The photo appears in the document at the location of the cursor. Tap it to close the menu.

7. You can tap on the image and use Cut, Copy, Delete, and Replace on the photo when it is selected. The latter option brings the photos menu back for you to select another.

8. Drag the blue dots around the photo to resize it.

9. While resizing, measurements appear next to the photo.

10. Tap the paintbrush button to bring up the Style and Arrange menu.

11. Tap Arrange to see options for flipping a photo, moving it in front of or behind other items on the page, and editing the mask of the photo.

12. Tap Edit Mask.

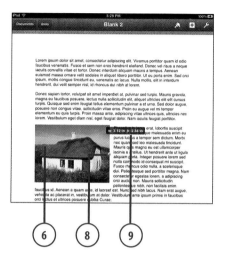

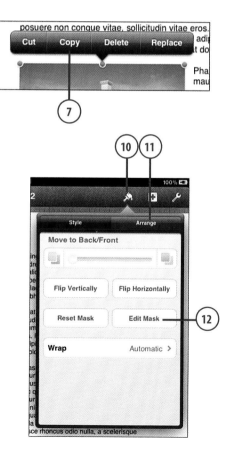

13. Drag the slider to resize the photo. The photo changes size, but the size of the object remains the same, which enables you to put the focus on a particular portion of the photo by moving the photo around inside the space. Tap Mask to finish.

14. Tap the Paintbrush icon to open the Style and Arrange menu again. Tap Wrap. Use the Wrap menu to designate how the text wraps around the photo and whether the photo should stay put on the page or move along as you insert text before it.

15. Tap Style.

16. Choose the type of border that you want to appear around the photo. There are six basic styles to choose from. In addition, you can tap Style Options and choose your own border and effects.

Rearranging Images

After you place an image in your document, you can drag it around and resize it as much as you want. Pages automatically snaps the edges of the image to the margins and center lines of the page as you drag it around.

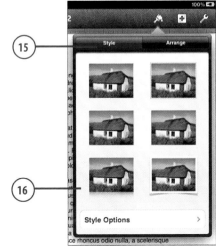

Importing Clipart

I've found that the best way to get clip art onto your iPad and into Pages is to drag it into iPhoto. Then, I create a ClipArt event to store the files in. I then sync my iPad, making sure that the ClipArt event is set to sync. You can also do this with a folder if you aren't using iPhoto or are on Windows.

Using Shapes in Documents

In addition to using clip art, you can also use some basic shapes in Pages. Inserting shapes works in the same basic manner.

1. Create a new document and add some text.

2. Tap the + button to bring up the Media/Tables/Charts/Shapes menu.

3. Tap the Shapes button.

4. Tap a shape, such as the rounded rectangle. It is placed in the middle of the text.

5. Tap the shape in the text to dismiss the menu.

6. Use the blue dots to resize the shape.

7. Tap and drag in the middle of the shape to move it around in the document.

8. Double-tap in the shape to enter text into the shape.

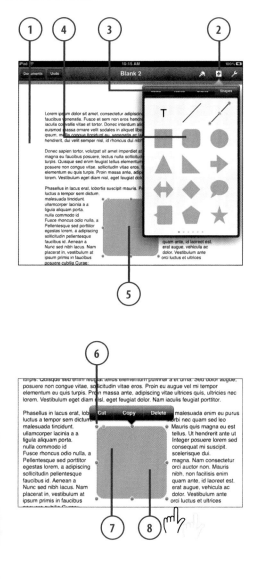

LOTS OF CHOICES

The first shape, shown with the letter T, is actually a hollow box where you can add text. The next choices are a line, an arrow, and then the shapes you can more easily see.

If you drag to the left, you can look through six pages of shape variations. These are the same shapes but with different borders, shading, or just outlines.

After you select a shape and add it to a document, you can always select it and press the paintbrush button to change its style to one of the other five. You can also choose Style Options and specify unique fills, borders, and effects for the shapes.

Creating Tables

Tables are a step up from using lists or tabs to format data in your documents. You can choose from several different types of tables, and entering data into them is relatively easy.

1. Start a new document.

2. Tap the + button.

3. Tap Tables. There are four different table options. In addition, you can swipe left and right in the menu to reveal six color variations.

4. Tap the first table to insert it.

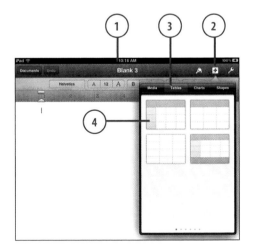

5. Tap the double arrow button to the right of the table or below the table to adjust the number of columns and rows.

6. Double-tap in a cell to enter text.

7. Tap the paintbrush button to bring up the Table/Headers/Cells menu.

8. Tap Table to choose from six table styles.

9. Tap Table Options to go to a menu that gives you even more control over the borders and background colors of the table. Tap the back arrow when done.

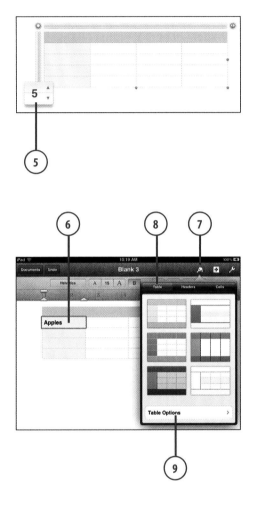

10. Tap Headers to change the number of rows used as a header and the number of columns as well. You can even add footer rows. These all show up as different colors according to the style of table.

11. Tap Arrange to bring up text wrapping options and to send the table behind or in front of other objects.

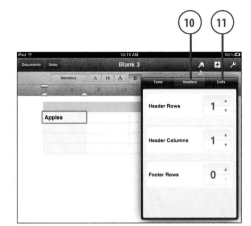

Moving Tables

When the table is selected and you see bars at the top and left and a circle at the top-left corner, you can drag the table around the document by grabbing it at any location and dragging.

Creating Charts

Charts are another way to express numbers visually. Pages supports nine different kinds of charts.

1. Create a blank document.

2. Tap the + button.

3. Tap Charts. You can look through six pages of chart styles, but the basics of each set of charts is the same.

4. Tap a chart to select it and insert that type of chart in the middle of your document.

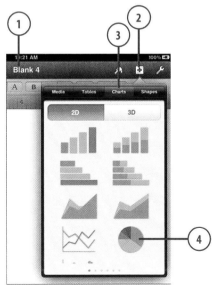

5. After selecting the chart, tap the
   Edit Data button.

6. Alter the existing data to create
   your own chart by tapping the
   field and typing.

7. When you finish entering data,
   tap Done.

8. When you return to the main
   document view, select the chart
   and tap the paintbrush button.

9. From the Chart menu, select a
   color scheme for the chart. You
   can also switch between 2D and
   3D versions of each style.

10. Tap Chart Options. Use the Chart
    Options menu to change a variety
    of properties of the chart.

11. For 3D charts, you can tap and
    drag in the middle of a chart to
    adjust its 3D angle.

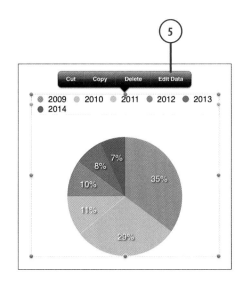

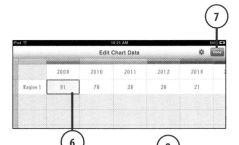

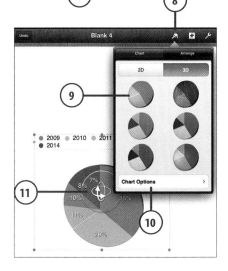

Document Setup

You can change a variety of your document's properties in Pages.

1. Open a document or create a new one.

2. Tap the Wrench button.

3. Choose Document Setup.

4. Drag the arrows at the four edges of the page to adjust the width and height of the page.

5. Tap in the header to add text to the header.

6. While typing in the header, tap in one of the three spaces (left, center, right) and you'll see a toolbar where you can select Page Numbers to have the page number automatically placed in that part of the header.

Add Background Images

One thing you can do with Document Setup that is not obvious is to add background objects that appear under every page. You can tap the + button and add photos, tables, charts, and shapes to the main page area. The image you add appears behind the text. You can even add text that appears on every page by just inserting a borderless, empty text box shape and adding text to it.

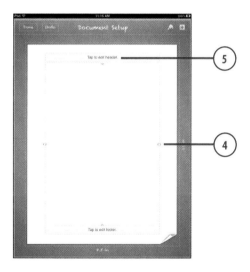

7. Tap the footer to add text to the footer.

8. Tap the page curl to change the paper size.

Create a Background

You can color the entire background by creating a square box and stretching it to fill the page. Then add a shaded or textured background to it as a color in the shape's Style Options. You can also place a picture over the entire background.

Sharing and Printing Documents

Thanks to iCloud, sharing documents with Pages, Numbers, and Keynote among your own devices is very easy. Any document you create on any device will simply be available to the others. But you can also share your document with another person by emailing it, printing it, or sending it to a network server.

1. While viewing a document, tap the tools button at the upper right.

2. Tap Share and Print.

3. Choose Email Document to send the document via email.

4. Choose the format in which to send the document. You can send it as a Pages document, a PDF, or a Microsoft Word document.

5. Choose Print to send the document to a network AirPrint printer.

6. You can export from Pages to a PDF or Word file and open it in other apps that can handle these file types. Numbers and Keynote can use this function to export into formats like Excel and PowerPoint.

7. Choose Copy to iTunes to place a copy of the document in a location of your iPad where you can see and transfer it using iTunes the next time you sync with your computer.

8. Choose this to send the document to an Internet file transfer service.

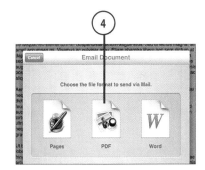

Pages Does Word

You can put more than just Pages documents into the iTunes list to import. Pages can also take Microsoft Word .doc and even .docx files.

Pages Is Not Pages

The Pages on your iPad and the Pages on your Mac are not the same. You can do a lot more with Pages on your Mac. So, sometimes you might receive a Document Import Warning message telling you what didn't work as you import your file to your iPad.

Design and enter data
into spreadsheets.

With Numbers you can create data spreadsheets, perform calculations, and create
forms and charts.

→ Creating a New Spreadsheet
→ Totaling Columns
→ Averaging Columns
→ Performing Calculations
→ Formatting Tables
→ Creating Forms
→ Creating Charts
→ Using Multiple Tables

Spreadsheets with Numbers

Numbers is a versatile program that enables you to create
the most boring table of numbers ever (feel free to try for the
world record on that one) or an elegant chart that illustrates a
point like no paragraph of text ever could.

Creating a New Spreadsheet

The way you manage documents in Numbers is exactly the same as you do in Pages, so if you need a refresher, refer to Chapter 11, "Writing with Pages." Let's jump right in to creating a simple spreadsheet.

1. Tap the Numbers icon on your Home screen to start.

2. Tap + and then Create Spreadsheet to see all the template choices.

3. Tap Blank to choose the most basic template.

Numbers Terminology

A grid of numbers is called a *table*. A page of tables, often just a single table taking up the whole page, is a *sheet*. You can have multiple sheets in a document, all represented by tabs. The first tab in this case represents "Sheet 1." Tap the + to add a new sheet.

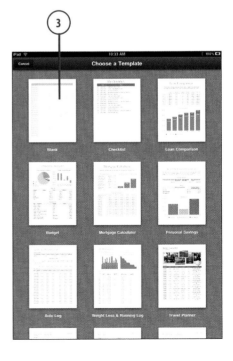

4. Tap in one of the cells to select the sheet. An outline appears around the cell.

5. Double-tap the cell this time. An on-screen keypad appears.

6. Use the keypad to type a number. The number appears in both the cell and a text field above the keypad. Use this text field to edit the text, tapping inside it to reposition the cursor if necessary.

7. Tap the upper next button, the one with the arrow pointing right.

Switching Keyboard Options

The four buttons just above and to the left of the keypad represent number, time, text, and formula formats for cells. If you select the number, you get a keypad to enter a number. If you select the clock, you get a special keypad to enter dates and times. If you select the T, you get a regular keyboard. Finally, if you select the equal sign (=), you get a keypad and special buttons to enter formulas.

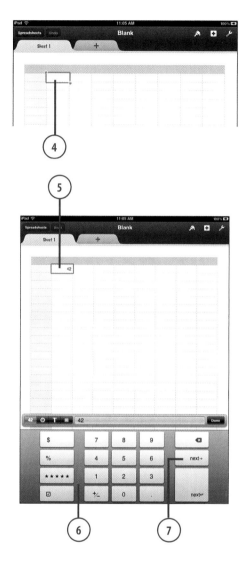

8. The cursor moves to the column in the next cell. Type a number here, too.

9. Tap the next button again and enter a third number.

10. Tap the space just above the first number you entered. The keypad changes to a standard keyboard to type text instead of numbers.

11. Type a label for this first column.

12. Tap in each of the other two column heads to enter titles for them as well.

13. Tap to the left of the first number you entered. Type a row title.

14. Now enter a few more rows of data.

15. Tap the Done button.

16. Tap and drag the circle with four dots in it to the right of the bar above the table. Drag it to the left to remove the unneeded columns.

17. Tap and drag the same circle at the bottom of the vertical bar to the left of the table. Drag it up to remove most of the extra rows, leaving a few for future use.

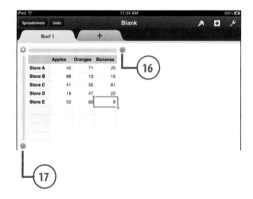

Totaling Columns

One of the most basic formula types is a sum. In the previous example, for instance, you might want to total each column.

1. Start with the result of the previous example. Double-tap in the cell just below the bottom number in the first column.

2. Tap the = button to switch to the formula keypad.

3. Tap the SUM button on the keypad.

4. The formula for the cell appears in the text field.

5. Tap the green check mark button.

6. The result of the formula appears in the cell. Repeat steps 2 through 4 for the other columns in the table.

Automatic Updates

If you are not familiar with spreadsheets, the best thing about them is that formulas like this automatically update. So if you change the number of Apples in Store C in the table, the sum in the last row automatically changes to show the new total.

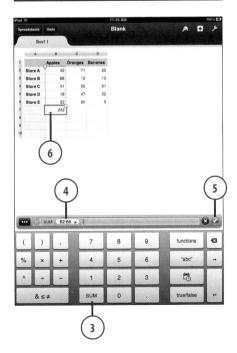

Averaging Columns

We lucked out a bit with the sum function because it has its own button. What about the hundreds of other functions? Let's start with something simple like column averages.

1. Continuing with the example from the previous section, double-tap on the cell below the total of the first column of numbers.

2. Tap the = button to switch to formula mode.

3. Tap the functions button.

4. Tap the Categories tab at the top of the menu, and tap Statistical from the Functions button menu.

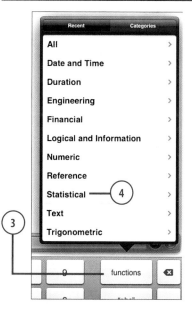

5. Tap AVERAGE from the list of functions.

6. Now you get AVERAGE(value) in the entry field. The light blue means the "value" is selected and ready to be defined.

7. Tap cell B2 (Apples for Store A).

8. Drag the bottom dot to include cells B2 through B6. Don't add the Total row to the average. The entry field should now read AVERAGE(B2:B6).

9. Tap the green check mark button.

10. The average of the column should now be in the cell. Tap it once to see the Cut/Copy/Paste menu.

11. Tap Copy.

12. Tap the cell below the total for the second column of numbers.

13. Drag the bottom-right dot to expand the area to cover the next cell as well.

14. Tap in the two cells to bring up the Paste option.

15. Tap Paste.

16. Tap Paste Formulas.

17. All three columns now show the average for rows 2 through 6. Notice how Numbers is smart enough to understand when you copy and paste a formula from one column to another, that it should look at the same rows but a different column.

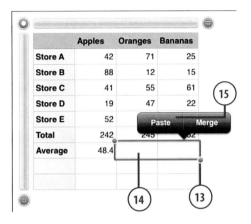

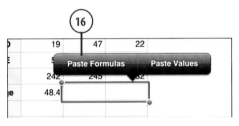

Performing Calculations

So far, we have seen two simple formulas. Let's see what else you can do with one of hundreds of different functions and the standard mathematical symbols.

1. Start with a table like this one. It shows the base and height measurements for three triangles.

2. Double-tap in the third column.

3. Tap the = button to enter a formula.

4. Tap the first number in the first column. "Base Triangle 1" should fill the entry field.

5. Tap the division symbol.

6. Tap the 2.

7. Tap the Multiplication button.

8. Tap the first number in the second column.

9. The entry field now reads "Base Triangle 1 ÷ 2 x Height Triangle 1."

10. Tap the green check mark.

11. You get the result of 10.5, which is half the base of the triangle times its height, or the area of the triangle.

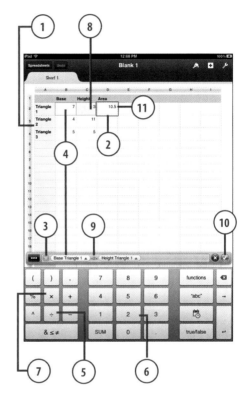

Using Parentheses

Note that a more careful mathematician would rather see it written "(Base Triangle 1 ÷ 2) × Height Triangle 1." By grouping the base divided by 2 inside parentheses, you guarantee the correct result. You can use the parentheses to do that in the formula keypad.

Formatting Tables

Let's move away from calculations to design. You have many formatting options to make your spreadsheets pretty.

Formatting Cells

1. Go back to the original example or something similar.

2. Select the six cells that make up the totals and average.

3. Tap the paintbrush button.

4. Tap Cells to see cell styling, formatting, and coloring choices.

5. Select Fill Color.

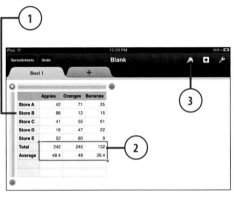

6. Tap the lightest shade of blue. You can also drag to the left to go to the second page of colors, which is actually a set of grays. The second page includes an option to reset the fill to the original style.

7. Tap the back arrow to go back to the Cells menu.

8. Tap B to make the text bold.

9. Change the selection to include only the row of averages.

10. Tap the paintbrush button again.

11. Tap Text Options.

12. Tap Color.

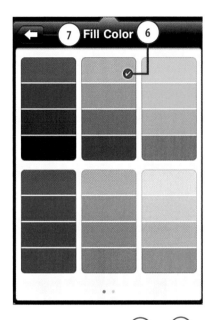

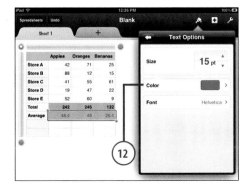

13. Choose the third darkest blue.

14. Tap the back arrow twice to go back two menus.

15. Tap Format.

16. Tap the blue arrow to the right of Number.

17. Set the number of decimal places. Try 2.

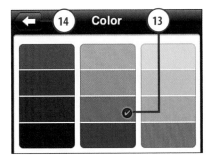

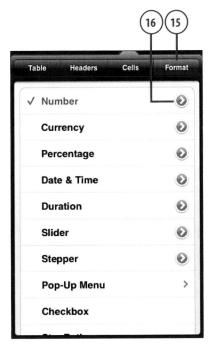

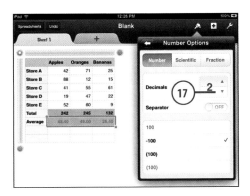

Formatting Whole Tables

Beyond just formatting cells, you can also use many options to change the basic style of your table. Let's explore some of the options.

1. Starting with the table from the previous example; tap anywhere in the table to select it.

2. Tap the paintbrush button to bring up the menu.

3. Tap Table.

4. Try a different style, like the greenish one on the left, second down.

5. The new style replaces the formatting we did for the cells, so it is best to find a table style before you customize the cell styles.

6. Tap the Table Options button to explore other table options.

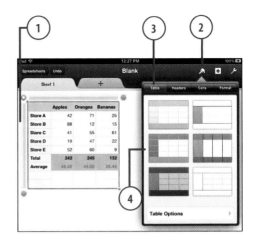

7. Tap the Table Name switch to add or remove the title.

8. Tap the Table Border switch to add or remove a border.

9. Tap the Alternating Rows switch to have the color of the rows alternate.

10. Tap Grid Options for more detailed control of the look of the grid used in the table.

11. Tap Text Size and Table Font to change the size and font used in the table.

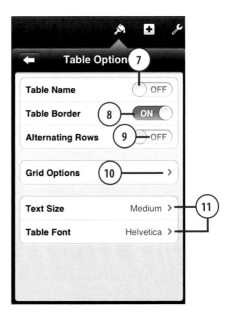

Using Headers and Footers

Let's continue with the previous example to explore headers and footers:

1. Tap the Back button to return to the main formatting menu.

2. Tap the Headers button to adjust the number of header rows and columns and add footer rows.

3. Tap the Footer Rows up arrow to increase the footer rows to 4.

Creating Forms

Forms are an alternative way to enter data in a spreadsheet. A form contains many pages, each page representing a row in a table. Let's continue with the previous example and use it to make a form.

1. Tap the + button, which looks like a second tab in the document.

2. Tap New Form. Note that in order to get the option to make a form, you need to have at least one column with a value in its header row.

3. Choose a table. We have only one, so the choice is simple. Tap Table 1 to see the first page in the form, which represents the first row of data from our table.

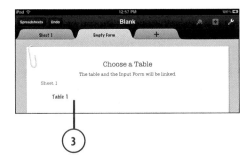

4. Tap the right arrow at the bottom of the screen to move through the five existing rows (pages) of data.

5. Tap the + button at the bottom of the screen to enter a new row of data.

6. Tap at the top of the screen to enter a row heading.

7. Tap in each of the three fields to enter data.

8. Use the next button on the on-screen keypad to move to the next field.

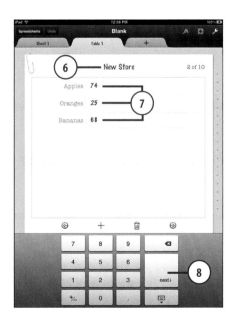

9. When you finish, tap the first tab, Sheet 1, to return to the original spreadsheet. You should see the new data in a new row.

	Apples	Oranges	Bananas
Store A	42	71	25
Store B	88	12	15
Store C	41	55	61
Store D	19	47	22
Store E	52	60	9
New Store	74	25	68
Total	242	245	132
Average	48.40	49.00	26.40

It's Not All Good

WHY DIDN'T THE FORMULAS UPDATE?

Unfortunately, the formulas for the totals and averages in our example did not update to use the new row. They both stuck with rows 2 through 7 of the table and did not expand to use row 8. What went wrong?

Well, first, if we had added a row in the middle of the table, it would have expanded the sum area. So part of our problem is that we added a cell below the sum area.

Second, we created the cell with the sum function in a regular cell. Then we turned it into a footer cell. If we start over by deleting that sum cell and creating it again, Numbers is smart enough to realize that we mean *all* the rows in the column between the header and footer. Instead of =SUM(B2:B7), we would simply get =SUM(B). Then we can add more rows using the form, and the sum would increase properly.

So, delete the formula from B9 and replace it with =SUM(B), and you are in business. Do the same with the other sum and average cells. When you do this, Numbers is smart enough to create the formula for you when you tap the SUM button. The formula is actually stated as =SUM(Apples) because we named the column Apples.

To create your Average row, use the Functions button and select AVERAGE as before, but tap the bar above columns B, C, and D to tell Numbers you want the average of the whole column between the header and footer.

Creating Charts

Representing numbers visually is one of the primary functions of a modern spreadsheet program. With Numbers, you can create bar, line, and pie charts and many variations of each.

1. Create a new blank spreadsheet and then fill it with some basic data to use as an example. Shrink the table to remove unneeded cells.

2. Tap the + button at the top of the screen.

3. Select Charts.

4. Page through six different chart color variations. Tap the chart at the top left.

5. You will now be asked to tap the chart and then select data from your spreadsheet.

6. Tap and drag over all the numbers in the body of your table to add all the rows of data to the table.

7. Tap Done.

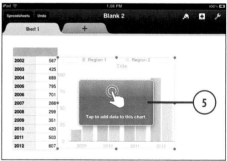

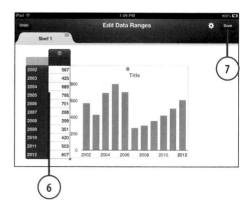

8. Tap and drag the chart and position it on the sheet.

9. Tap on the chart to make sure it is selected.

10. Tap the paintbrush button. Notice that you can alter all sorts of properties using the Chart/X Axis/Y Axis and Arrange menu.

11. Tap Chart Options.

12. Tap Chart Type.

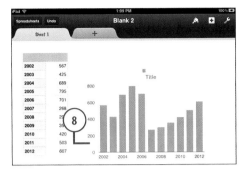

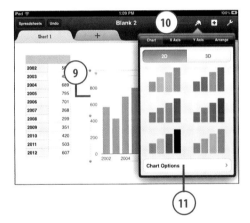

13. Tap Line to change the chart type to a line graph.

14. Tap outside the menu to dismiss it.

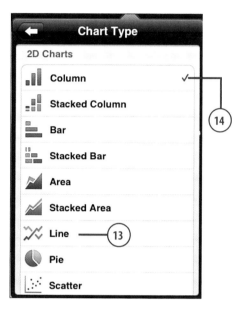

Using Multiple Tables

The primary way Numbers differs from spreadsheet programs such as Excel is that Numbers emphasizes page design. A Numbers sheet is not meant to contain just one grid of numbers. In Numbers, you can use multiple tables.

1. Create a new, blank spreadsheet and fill it with data as in the example image.

2. Shrink the table to remove any unneeded cells.

3. Select the cells in the body.

4. Tap the paintbrush button.

5. Tap Format.

6. Tap Currency.

7. Tap outside the menu to dismiss it.

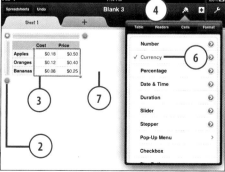

8. Tap the table to select it. Make sure just the table as a whole is selected, not a cell.

Selecting a Table

It can be difficult to select an entire table without selecting a cell. Tap in a cell to select it. Then tap the circle that appears in the upper-left corner of the table to change your selection to the entire table.

9. Tap the paintbrush button.

10. Tap Table Options.

11. Tap the Table Name switch to give the table a name.

12. Tap outside the menu to dismiss it.

13. Select just the table name and change it.

14. Tap the + button.

15. Tap Tables.

16. Select the first table type.

17. Enter the data as shown and shrink the table to remove any unneeded cells.

18. Select the table title and change it.

Clean Up the Formatting

To keep this tutorial short, I left some things out. For instance, you can select the date columns and change the formatting. Obviously each row represents a month. So, you don't need the full date, including the day. You can change the date format of those columns to one that doesn't include the day, only the month and year. Just select those cells and tap the paintbrush button and look under Format. Select Date & Time and tap the blue circle to choose a specific date and time format.

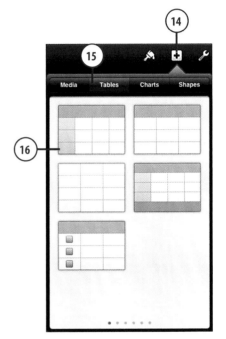

Cost and Price

	Cost	Price
Apples	$0.18	$0.50
Oranges	$0.12	$0.40
Bananas	$0.08	$0.25

Inventory Received

	Apples	Oranges	Bananas
Jan 1, 2010	50	0	0
Feb 1, 2010	50	100	200
Mar 1, 2010	0	200	0
Apr 1, 2010	50	0	200

19. Select the entire second table.

20. Tap the Copy button.

21. Tap outside the table in a new location in the sheet.

22. Tap Paste.

23. Change the title and contents of the new table as shown.

24. Now select the second and third tables and expand them with one extra column each, as shown.

iPad 🛜   7:17 PM

My Spreadsheets   Undo   **Blank 3**

Sheet 1   **+**

Cost and Price

	Cost	Price
Apples	$0.18	$0.50
Oranges	$0.12	$0.40
Bananas		

Cut   Copy   Delete

Inventory Received

	Apples	Oranges	Bananas
Jan 1, 2010	50	0	0
Feb 1, 2010	50	100	200
Mar 1, 2010	0	200	0
Apr 1, 2010	50	0	200

Inventory Received

	Apples	Oranges	Bananas
Jan 1, 2010	50	0	0
Feb 1, 2010	50	100	200
Mar 1, 2010	0	200	0
Apr 1, 2010	50	0	200

Select All   Paste

Inventory Received

	Apples	Oranges	Bananas	Cost
Jan 1, 2010	50	0	0	
Feb 1, 2010	50	100	200	
Mar 1, 2010	0	200	0	
Apr 1, 2010	50	0	200	

Inventory Sold

	Apples	Oranges	Bananas	Revenue
Jan 1, 2010	23	15	42	
Feb 1, 2010	22	20	37	
Mar 1, 2010	19	21	40	
Apr 1, 2010	27	18	42	

25. Double-tap in the first cell under Cost.

26. Tap on the = button next to the entry field to enter a formula.

27. Tap the Apples cell for the first row.

28. Tap × in the on-screen keyboard, and tap the cost of apples from the Cost and Price table.

29. Tap +.

30. Tap the Oranges cell and then tap × again. Then tap the cost of oranges and again tap +.

31. Tap the Bananas cell. Then tap × and tap the cost of bananas.

32. Tap the part of the formula that reads Cost Apples.

33. Turn on all four preservation switches to prevent the cell reference from changing as we copy and paste. We want the amount of inventory to change with each row, but the price from the other table remains the same.

34. Repeat steps 32 and 33 for the cost of oranges and the cost of bananas in the formula.

35. Tap the green check mark to complete the formula.

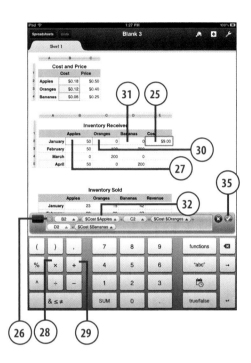

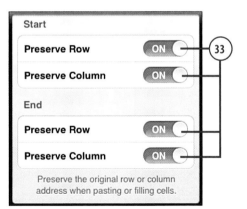

36. Tap the paintbrush button.

37. Change the format of the cell to Currency.

38. Copy that cell and paste it in to the three below it. When prompted, choose to Paste Formulas not Values.

The result is that you have a calculation based on data from two tables. You can complete this spreadsheet for practice, if you want. Create a similar formula for the revenue column of the next table, based on the price of each item and the amount sold.

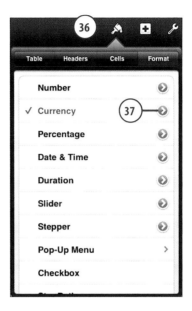

Enhance the Sheet

Another thing you can do is to add more titles, text, and images to the sheet—even shapes and arrows. These not only make the sheet look nice, but can also act as documentation as a reminder of what you need to do each month—or instruct someone else what to do to update the sheet.

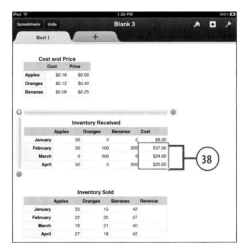

Create and display business and
educational presentations.

In this chapter, we use Keynote to build and
display presentations.

Presentations with Keynote

You can't have a suite of business apps without having
a Presentation tool, and Keynote is that tool on the iPad.
The basics of using Keynote are the same as for Pages and
Numbers. So let's get right to making presentations.

Building a Simple Presentation

Keynote works only in horizontal screen orientation. So after you launch Keynote, turn your iPad on its side. The way you manage documents in Keynote is exactly the same as you do in Pages and Numbers, including the ability to use iCloud to store your documents. If you need a refresher, refer to Chapter 11, "Writing with Pages."

1. Tap the Keynote icon on the Home screen. If this is the first time you are using Keynote, the sample presentation should be front and center. If so, tap the Presentations button at the top left to get to your list of presentations first, and then you'll find the + button.

2. Tap the + button to create a new presentation.

3. Tap Create Presentation.

4. Choose a theme. We use Gradient for the task.

5. Double-tap the line of text that reads Double-tap to edit.

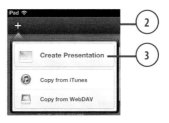

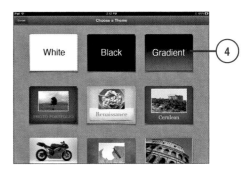

6. Type a title using the on-screen keyboard.

7. Double-tap the subtitle area and type a subtitle.

8. Tap the Close Keyboard button.

9. Tap the small button in the bottom-right corner of the picture to open a photo albums browser.

10. Choose a photo.

11. Tap the large + button at the bottom-left corner to bring up a list of slides.

12. Tap any of the slides templates to add a slide. You now have two slides in your presentation.

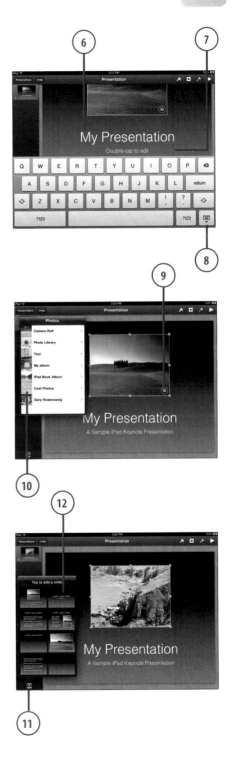

STARTING NEW PRESENTATIONS

Keynote presentations are made up of slides. The slides in the current presentation are shown at the left of the screen. The selected slide takes up most of the screen. The slides are built from one of eight slide templates, which you can modify as needed.

Be aware that there is no way to switch themes or to access the design of another theme after you start a new presentation. If you're used to working with Keynote on a Mac, you might be disappointed by this.

You can copy and paste entire slides between presentation documents, though. So if you want a document that mixes themes, you can achieve it by copying and pasting.

Building Your Own Slide

You can remove items and add your own to any template. You can practice adding your own elements to a slide by using the blank template.

1. Start a new document or continue from the previous example. Tap + to add a new slide.

2. Choose the blank slide to the lower right.

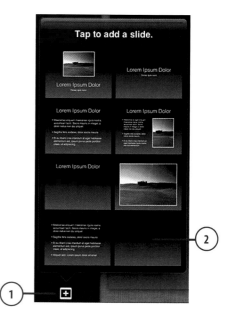

3. Tap the + button at the top to add an element.

4. Tap Media.

5. Select an album, and then select a photo from that album.

6. With the photo selected, grab one of the blue dots and shrink the image.

7. With the image selected, tap the paintbrush button and then tap Style.

8. Tap the bottom right of the six basic image styles or tap Style Options to customize the look of the photo even more.

Select All

To select all objects, tap a space with no objects. After a short delay, tap there again, and then you can choose Select All.

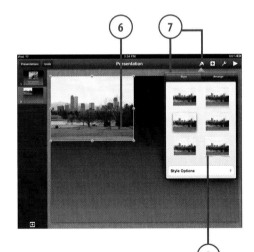

9. Add two more images using steps 3 through 8.

10. To select multiple items, use two fingers. Tap the first image with one finger and hold it. Use a second figure to tap the other two images to add them to the selection. Then drag all three images into a better position.

11. Tap the + button to add another element.

Tables and Charts Anyone?

You can also add tables and charts, even basic shapes, in the same way you would do it in Pages. There are a lot of similarities between using Pages and using Keynote.

12. Tap Shapes.

13. Tap the first element, a T, which represents a plain text box.

14. Tap outside the menu to dismiss it.

15. Tap the text box to select it.

16. Drag it to a new position and expand it.

17. Double-tap in the text box to enter some text.

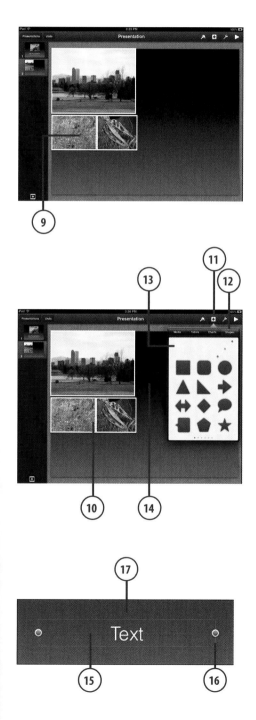

18. Close the keyboard and select the text box. With the text box selected, tap the paintbrush button.

19. Tap Text to change the font style.

20. Make the text bold by tapping B.

21. Tap outside the menu to dismiss it.

22. Your text is now bold.

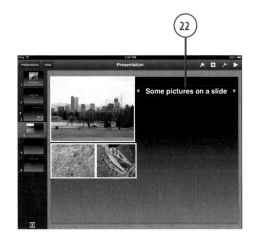

Adding Transitions

Just like other presentation programs, Keynote on iPad has a number of transition options. To practice working with transitions, start with a sample presentation, such as the one we have been working on, or create a new document with some sample slides.

1. Select the first slide on the left.

2. Tap the Transitions button that should appear.

3. Scroll through the transitions and pick one. Try Blinds. The slide animates to show you the transition. It then returns.

4. Tap Options.

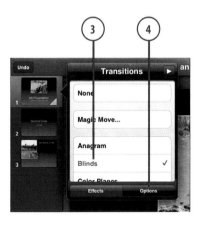

5. Select any options associated with the transition. For example, the Blinds transition can move in any of four directions. If you don't want to change any options, tap elsewhere to dismiss the menu.

6. Tap Done in the upper-right corner of the screen.

Magic Move

Another type of transition is the Magic Move. This is where objects on one slide are the same as the objects on the next, but they are in different positions. The transition between the slides moves these objects from the first position to the second.

1. Select a slide with several objects on it, such as three images. Tap the Transitions button.

2. Tap the transition.

3. Choose Magic Move.

Unique Effects with Magic Move

The great thing about the Magic Move transition is that you can create some unique effects. For instance, in the example, I could bunch all the photos into a tiny space on the first slide and then spread them out in the second slide. The transition would make it seem like the photos are bursting out and falling into place.

4. Tap Yes to duplicate the current slide so that you have two identical slides from which to create the Magic Move transition.

5. Slides 3 and 4 are identical, and slide 4 is the current slide. Move the objects around to reposition them or resize them. The stars indicate which elements are taking part in the magic move.

6. Tap the third frame.

7. Tap the play arrow to preview the transition from slide 3 to slide 4. You will need to tap the screen then to proceed from the 3rd slide to the 4th one and see the transition.

8. Tap Done in the upper-right corner of the screen.

Object Transitions

In addition to the entire screen trans-
forming from one slide to the next,
you can also define how you want
individual elements on the slide to
appear.

1. Start off with a slide that includes
   a title and a bullet list. Tap the
   slide's title text.

2. Tap Animate.

3. Tap the build in button.

4. Tap Blast to see a preview of the
   animation. You can also explore
   the Options, Delivery, and Order
   parts of the menu, but for this
   task we leave those settings alone.

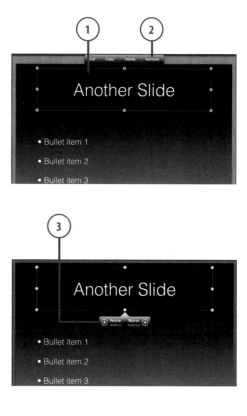

5. Tap the bullet list.

6. Tap build in.

7. Scroll down to Move In and tap it.

8. Tap Delivery.

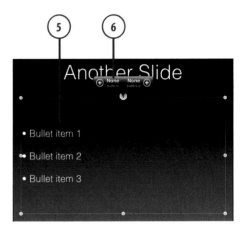

Don't Build the First Object

A common mistake is to set every object to build, as we have in this example. Because the first object, the title, builds in, it means that nothing appears on the slide at first. You start off blank. Then the title appears and then the bullet items. Sometimes, though, you should start a slide with the title already on it.

9. Tap By Bullet and then tap Done in the upper-right corner of the screen. The effect works by first showing you a blank screen, and then when you tap the screen, the title appears with the Blast transition. Each of your next three taps makes a bullet appear.

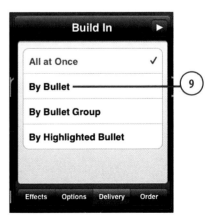

Organizing Slides

As you create presentations on your iPad, you might discover you need to re-order your slides, but that's no problem with Keynote. To practice, use a presentation that has several slides.

1. Create a presentation that includes several slides.

2. Tap and hold the third slide. It grows slightly larger and begins to follow your finger so that you can drag it down into another position.

Grouping Slides

There are two options when you drag a slide and place it back in the list. The first is to place it flush left, where it inserts normally. If you move the slide slightly to the right, though, you are grouping the slide with the one above it. Groups are a great way to put slides that belong together as a single element. That way, you can move them as one unit if you need to. To move them as a group, you close the group by tapping the triangle next to the parent slide. Then move the parent slide around, and all children come with it.

3. Drag slide 4 to the right so it inserts in a group owned by slide 3.

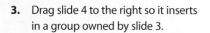

4. Tap the triangle on the left of slide 3 to close the group.

5. Tap slide 5 with your finger and continue to hold.

6. Use your other hand to tap slide 6 and then release your finger. You can now move this group of two slides as one unit.

7. Tap once to select a slide. Then tap a second time after a short delay to bring up a menu.

8. Use Cut, Copy, and Paste as you would while editing text. You can duplicate slides this way.

9. Tap Delete to remove a slide.

10. Tap Skip to mark a slide as one to skip during the presentation. This comes in handy when you want to remove a slide from a presentation temporarily, perhaps while presenting to a specific audience.

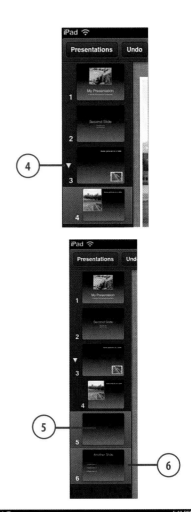

Playing Your Presentation

After you create your presentation, or if you want to preview what you've done, you can play your presentation.

1. With a presentation open in Keynote, tap the Play button.

2. The presentation fills the screen. Tap on the center or right side of the screen to advance to the next slide. You can also tap and drag from left to right.

3. To go back to the previous slide, drag right to left.

4. Tap on the left edge of the screen to bring up a list of slides.

5. Tap one of the items in the list to go directly to that slide.

6. Double-tap in the list of slides to dismiss the list.

7. Double-tap in the center of the screen to end the presentation and return to editing mode.

WHICH VIDEO ADAPTER?

One way to get Keynote's presentation out to an external screen is to use an adapter. There are two main choices: the VGA adapter or the HDMI adapter. Get the VGA adapter if you plan to present over a traditional meeting room projector. However, newer televisions and maybe some advanced projectors would use an HDMI connection. You can also convert VGA to fit other video connections. For instance, if you need to connect to a TV using a component or s-video, you should find some VGA adapters that work. See if you can find one that has been verified to work with an iPad before buying.

Presenting on an External Display

Presenting on your iPad with people looking over your shoulder probably isn't your goal. You want to present on a large monitor or a projector, which you can do with an iPad Dock Connector to VGA Adapter (see Chapter 18, "iPad Accessories," for more information).

1. When you have your VGA adapter connected, the Play button has a box around it to indicate that your iPad is ready to present on an external video device. Tap the Play button.

2. Tap in the middle or right side of the screen to move forward to the next slide or build the next object on the current slide.

3. Tap the left edge of the screen to bring up a list of slides.

4. Tap on one of the slides on the left to jump to it.

5. Tap the X button to stop the presentation.

6. Tap the Layouts button to bring up different layout options. You can choose to view both the current slide and next slide or the current slide with your slide notes at the bottom.

7. Tap and hold your finger on the slide to bring up a red dot that you can use as a pointer.

Presenting with Apple TV

You can also use the AirPlay ability of an Apple TV (2nd generation or newer) to send your presentation to a TV wirelessly. See "Using AirPlay to Play Music and Video on Other Devices" in Chapter 4 to set up AirPlay mirroring. But when you tap the Play button to play your presentation, mirroring will go into a special mode with the actual presentation on the TV and your presenter layout on your iPad's screen so you can control the slides.

Search for locations or get
directions with Maps.

In this chapter, you learn to use the Maps app to find locations and get directions.

→ Finding a Location
→ Searching for Places and Things
→ Getting Directions
→ Setting Bookmarks
→ Using Views
→ Getting Traffic Reports

Navigating with Maps

The Maps app is a great way to plan a trip—whether you're going to the grocery store or across the country. Maps in iOS 6 is a complete overhaul of the app, which previously showed Google maps. Apple now has its own mapping system. If you've used the old Maps app, you'll find this one familiar in how it works and where the controls are located, but the maps themselves look very different.

Finding a Location

The simplest thing you can probably do with Maps is to find a location.

1. Tap the Maps app on your Home screen.

2. Tap in the Search or Address field.

3. Type the name of a place.

4. Tap the Search button on the on-screen keyboard.

What Can You Search For?

You can search for a specific address. You can also use a general time or the name of a place or person, and Maps does the best it can to locate it. For example, you can try three-letter airport codes, landmark names, street intersections, and building names. The search keeps in mind your current Maps view, so if you search for a general area first, such as Denver, CO, and then for a building name, it attempts to find the building in Denver before looking elsewhere in the world.

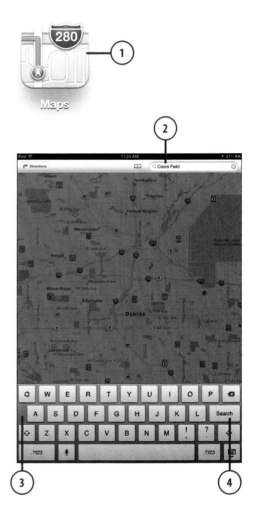

5. The map shifts to that location and zooms in.

6. Tap the i button next to the location name to get more information.

7. Use the Add to Contacts button to add the name, address, phone number, and other information to your Contacts app.

8. Use the Add to Bookmarks button to add the location as a bookmark in the Maps app.

9. Tap Reviews to read reviews of the location, assuming the location is a business or something else that has reviews on Yelp.

10. Tap outside the information area and try dragging and pinching to get a feel for using Maps.

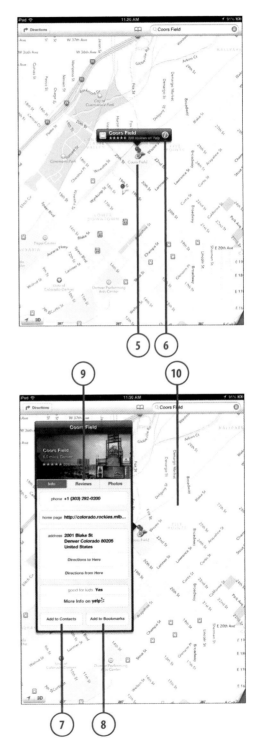

Where Am I?

Want to quickly center the map on your current location? Tap the GPS button (it looks like a small arrow) at the bottom-left corner of the screen. Even if your iPad doesn't have a GPS receiver, it takes a good guess as to your current location based on the local Wi-Fi networks it can see.

Searching for Places and Things

You can also use Maps to search for something that has more than one location. For instance, you could search for one location of your favorite computer store.

1. Start in Maps. You should see the last area you were viewing. If it is not your current location, search for that location or press the GPS button to go there.

2. Tap the search field and enter the name of a store.

3. Red pins appear on the map for all locations matching the search term in the general area. You might also see some dots representing other potential locations. Pinch to zoom in or out to see a wider area.

4. Tap a red pin to get the name of the location and an i button for more info.

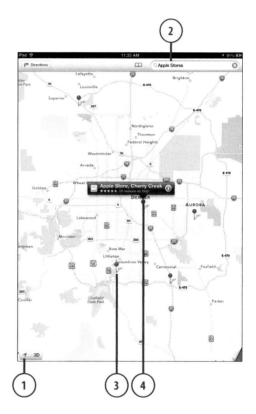

Sometimes Being General Is Good

Don't always restrict yourself to specific names such as "Apple store." You can type in general terms such as "coffee" or "restaurant" to get a broader selection of results.

Sometimes It Gets It Wrong

The maps database is huge, which means it also contains errors. Sometimes an address is wrong or the information is out of date, so you find yourself in front of a shoe shop instead of your favorite restaurant.

Siri: Finding Map Locations

You can ask Siri to find locations without even being in the Maps app. A small map will appear in the Siri interface, and you can tap on it to open up the Maps app, centered on that location. Try commands like:

"Where is Coors Field?"
"Show me Broadway and First Avenue on the map."
"Map 6th and Colorado Boulevard."

Getting Directions

The new iOS Maps app has something that the previous Maps app did not: turn-by-turn directions. If you are stationary, you'll need to settle for a map and a list of turns. But if you have a wireless mobile connection, you can use your iPad like a car's navigation system with spoken instructions.

1. In Maps, tap the Directions button. At this point, you may be asked to confirm whether the Maps app is allowed to use your current location.

2. Two fields appear at the top. The left field is already filled in with your current location. Change the location by tapping the X in the field to clear it and typing a new address.

3. Tap in the second field and type the destination location. Suggestions appear underneath in a list. You can tap a suggestion to fill that into the destination box.

4. Select the mode of transportation. You can get directions for driving, walking, or public transportation.

5. Tap the Route button.

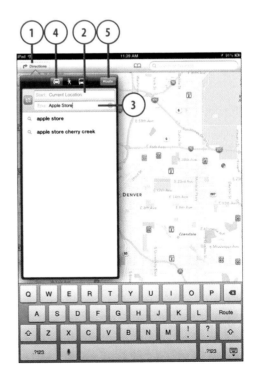

6. The directions show up as a blue line on the map. You might need to pinch to zoom out to see the whole route.

7. Alternate routes may also appear. Tap any route label to switch to that route.

8. Tap the Start button to go through the route turn-by-turn.

9. The current instruction appears at the top of the screen.

10. Tap on the next instruction to jump to it, or it will automatically shift over to the left as you accomplish the previous instruction. You can also swipe left to right to view future instructions.

11. Tap Overview to temporarily go to the map view that shows the entire route.

12. When you are done using the directions feature, tap End to exit back into normal map mode.

13. Tap the list button to view the directions as a simpler text list.

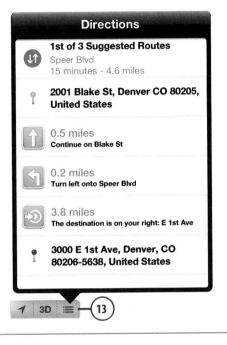

More Complex Routes

Sadly, the Maps app won't let you have more than two waypoints for a route. And you can't tap in the middle of a route. An alternative is to use Google maps in the Safari browser at http://maps.google.com.

Spoken Turn-By-Turn Directions

For those who have a wireless mobile connection on their iPad, directions become much more useful. You can use your mobile connection as you drive and the Maps app will follow along, updating the steps in your route as you make progress. You even get spoken directions as you approach each turn, so you don't need to take your eyes off the road.

 ## Siri: Getting Directions

The easiest way to get the Maps app to show you directions is to ask Siri. With or without the Maps app open, try phrases like:

"How do I get to Denver International Airport?"
"Take me to the nearest coffee shop."
"Plot a course to Colfax Avenue and Colorado Boulevard."
"Take me home."

Setting Bookmarks

If you find yourself requesting directions to or from the same location often, you might want to set a bookmark for that spot.

1. In Maps, search for a location.

2. Tap the i button to bring up the info box on that location.

3. Tap Add to Bookmarks.

4. Edit the name for the location if you want.

5. Tap Save.

6. Tap the Bookmarks button at the top of the screen to view your bookmarks.

7. At the bottom of the Bookmarks menu, tap Recents or Contacts to see a list of recently visited locations or pull up the address stored for a contact.

8. Tap the name of a bookmark to go to that location on the map.

9. You can also tap Edit to remove bookmarks.

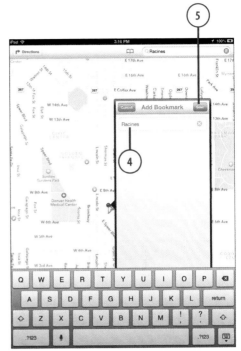

Add a Bookmark Manually

You can also create a bookmark by manually dropping a pin on the map. Tap and hold any location on the map, and a purple pin appears there. You can then drag the pin to another location if it isn't placed exactly where you want it. These pins have addresses and an i button just like any searched-for location. So, you can use the Add to Bookmarks button after tapping the i to add it as a bookmark. This comes in handy when the app doesn't quite get the address right.

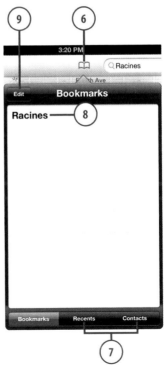

Using Views

One of the coolest things about online maps are the satellite and street views. Both are fun and helpful and a lot more interesting than a traditional map.

Using Satellite View

Satellite view is like the standard Map view in that you can search for places and get directions. But you can also get a better sense of what is at a location.

1. In Maps, tap the bottom-right corner, where the map page is curled a bit.

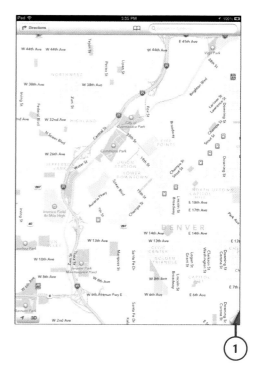

2. Tap Satellite to see a satellite view of your location. If that view isn't quite what you need, select Hybrid to see a satellite view that also gives you map references to identify items on the map.

3. Unpinch in the center of the map to zoom in.

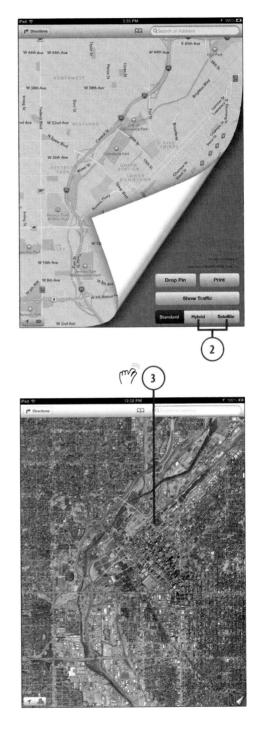

4. The closer view helps show you what the streets actually look like.

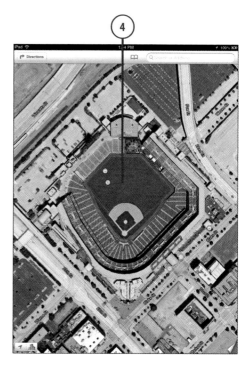

Using 3D View

The old Google Maps had street view, a way to view images taken at street level. However, the new Apple Maps app replaces that with 3D aerial views—images taken from airplanes that include all sides of buildings in major downtown areas.

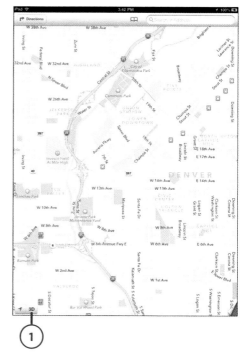

1. Start by looking in Maps using the standard view. Tap the 3D button.

2. The flat top-down view is replaced by a perspective view. Pinch to zoom in closer.

3. Larger buildings in downtown areas are now 3D objects. Use two fingers to rotate the image, and you can see the buildings from all angles.

4. Tap the bottom-right corner and then select Satellite view. You can still zoom and rotate in satellite view, even getting so close to the ground that you can virtually move between buildings.

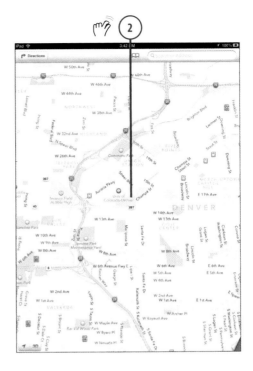

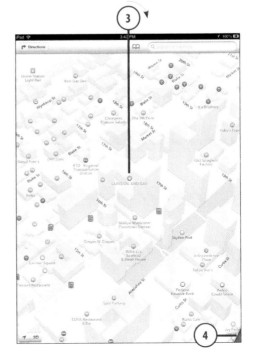

5. Tap to turn off 3D mode and
    return to standard top-down flat
    mode.

Not in My Town

Although 3D view is great for
those of us who live in big cities,
it isn't available for every location.
For there to be 3D models and
textures, an Apple-hired airplane
has to take pictures of your city.
They have gotten a lot of the
world's major cities, but not everywhere yet.

Getting Traffic Reports

The Maps app includes a way for you to see up-to-date traffic flow and information.

1. Bring up a Map view that shows
    some highways and major
    boulevards.

2. Tap the page corner.

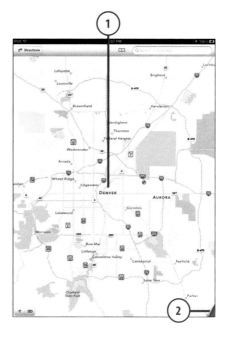

3. Turn on Traffic overlays.

4. The map shows red and yellow dashed lines where traffic is slow.

5. There are also icons for accidents, road closures, and construction. Tap any of these for details.

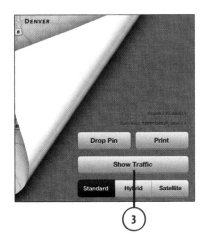

Siri: Traffic Reports

You can quickly bring up the map with traffic reports turned on by asking Siri:

What's the traffic like?
What's the traffic like in San Francisco?

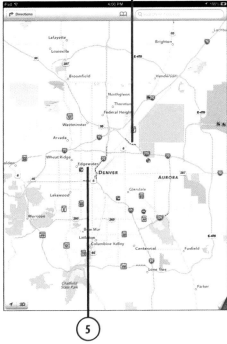

Search Apple's App Store for thousands of useful, educational, and entertaining apps.

To go beyond the basic functionality of your iPad, you need to learn how to add more apps using the App Store.

The World of Apps

Apps that come with your iPad and the iWork suite are just the tip of the iceberg. The App Store contains thousands of apps from third-party developers, with more added each day.

You use the App Store app to shop for and purchase new apps—although many are free. You can also rearrange the app icons on your Home screen pages to organize them.

Purchasing an App

Adding a new app to your iPad requires that you visit the App Store. You do that, not surprisingly, with the App Store app on your Home screen.

1. Tap the App Store icon on your Home screen.

2. You see the featured apps at the top of the screen.

3. Swipe left or right in the New and Noteworthy section to view more featured apps. You can do the same for the sections below, which often change to feature different types of apps.

4. Scroll down to see more featured apps.

5. Tap Top Charts to see the top paid apps and top free apps.

6. Tap More to see a list of app categories.

7. Tap any category to go to the page of featured apps in that category.

8. Use the search box to search for an app by keyword.

9. The switch at the top lets you filter between iPad apps and iPhone apps. Apps that are optimized to work well with both screen sizes will appear in both.

10. Select whether you want to see apps that are free, paid, or both.

11. Select a category to narrow down the search results.

12. Choose how you want the results to be ordered: relevance, popularity, ratings, or release date.

13. Tap an app to read more about it.

Redeem Codes

If you go to the bottom of any listings page in the App Store, you will see a button marked Redeem. Use this to enter any redemption code you get for a free app. You may get a code because someone sends you an app as a gift. Developers also send out a handful of these codes when they release a new app or app version.

Automatically Download New Apps

If you go to the Settings app, look for the iTunes & App Store category. There you can turn on automatic downloads for apps, as well as music and books. Once you turn this on, purchasing an app on your Mac or PC in iTunes, or on another iOS device with the same Apple ID, will automatically send this app to your iPad as well.

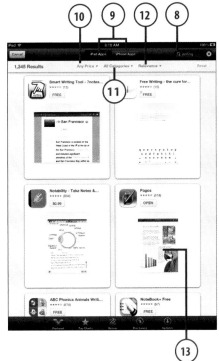

14. The app's page displays screen-shots, other apps by the same company, and user reviews.

15. Tap on the price on the left under the large icon to purchase an app. It changes to a Buy App button. Tap it again. If you have already purchased the app, the button will simply say "Open" and you can launch the app by tapping the button.

16. Scroll down to read the descrip-tion of the app.

17. Tap here to look at ratings and reviews for the app.

18. Scroll left and right to flip through the screenshots for the app.

19. When you purchase an app, it starts installing, and you can watch the progress from the app's information page in the App Store app or from the location of the app's icon on your Home screen.

Redownloading an App You Already Purchased

Once you buy an app, you own it forever—at least as long as you keep using the same Apple ID. At the bot-tom of the App Store app, you see a button marked "Purchased." Tap that to see a list of all apps you have bought, even if you have removed them from this iPad, or maybe never even downloaded them in the first place. Perhaps you previously bought an app on your iPhone or iPod Touch. You can quickly jump to any of these apps and download them to your iPad without paying for it a second time.

Arranging Apps on Your iPad

It doesn't take long to have several pages of apps. Fortunately, you can rearrange your app icons in two ways. The first is to do it on the iPad.

1. Tap and hold an icon until all the icons start to jiggle.

2. The icon you are holding is a little larger than the others. Drag it and drop it in a new location. To carry the icon to the next page of apps, drag it to the right side of the screen.

3. Delete an app from your iPad by tapping the X at the upper left of the icon. Note that the X does not appear over all apps, as the default set of apps that come with your iPad cannot be removed.

Deleting Is Not Forever

If you sync your iPad to iTunes on a computer, you do not delete apps forever. All apps remain in your iTunes library on your computer unless you remove them. So, you can get rid of the app from your iPad and find it is still on your computer if you want to select it to sync back to your iPad. Additionally, you can always redownload an app from the app store that you purchased previously, without paying again. If you don't think you'll need an app for a while, you can delete it and then add it back again later.

4. When finished, press the Home button.

WHAT ELSE CAN I DO?

Here are a few more tips that might make your app housekeeping easier:

- You can release an app and then grab another to move it. If the apps still jiggle, you can keep moving app icons.

- You can drag apps into and out of the dock along the bottom where you can fit up to six apps. Apps in the dock appear on all pages of your Home screen.

- You can drag an app to the right on the last page of apps to create a new page of your Home screen.

Arranging Apps with iTunes

You can also arrange your apps when you sync with iTunes on your Mac or PC. Simply select the iPad in the left sidebar of your iTunes window, and then select Apps on the right. You can move apps between screens and also decide which apps get synced between your computer and your iPad.

Creating App Folders

In addition to spreading your apps across multiple pages, you can also group them together in folders so that several apps take up only one icon position on a screen.

1. Identify several apps that you want to group together. Tap and hold one of those apps until the icons start to jiggle.

2. Continue to hold your finger down, and drag the icon to another one you wish to group it with.

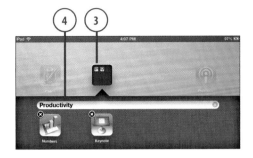

3. An app folder appears, and all other app icons should fade so you can focus on your new app folder.

4. Change the name of the app folder.

5. Press the Home button once to dismiss the name editor, and again to return to your home screen.

6. You now see the app folder on your home screen. You can drag other apps to this folder using steps 1 and 2.

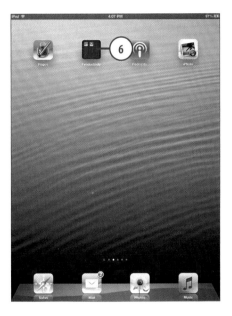

After you have created an app folder, you can access the apps in it by first tapping on the folder and then tapping the app you want to launch. Tapping and holding any app in the folder gives you the opportunity to rename the folder, rearrange the icons in the folder, or drag an app out of the folder.

Viewing Currently Running Apps

You can have many apps running at once on your iPad. In fact, after you launch an app, it will remain running by default even if you switch back to the home screen and run another app. Apps running in the background use little or no resources. You can think of them as paused apps. You can switch back to them at any time, and most apps will resume right where you left off.

1. Double-press the Home button. This brings up the list of recent apps at the bottom of the screen.

2. You can flick back and forth to view apps further down the list.

3. Tap an app to return to it.

4. Press the Home button to simply exit the list.

5. If you flick to the right, until you get all the way to the left end of the recent apps list, you will get to controls for the audio app you are currently using, such as the Music app.

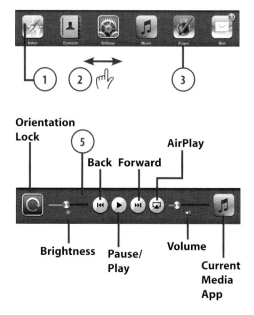

Moving from App to App with a Gesture

If you have several apps running, you can quickly move between them by using four-finger gestures. Just swipe left or right with four fingers at the same time. This will move you from app to app without needing to go back to the Home screen, or use the list of recent apps.

Quitting Apps

Although it is rarely necessary to completely quit an app, you can do it in one of two ways. This will force the app to shut down if it has frozen, or if you simply want to start the app fresh to see an introduction sequence or work around problems the app may be having.

1. Press the home button once to leave the app and return to the Home Screen.

2. Double-press the button to bring up the list of recent apps at the bottom of the screen.

3. Tap and hold any of the app icons in the list until they all start to jiggle and the red circle minus button appears in the upper-left corner of each.

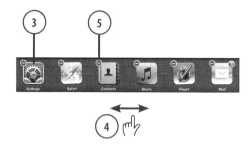

4. Swipe left or right to locate the app you want to quit.

5. Tap the red circle minus button above the app that you want to quit.

A second method works when the app is the one currently on the screen.

1. Press and hold the wake/sleep button on the top of your iPad for about 3 seconds. You will see the "Slide to power off" control appear.

2. Don't use the "Slide to power off" control or press the Cancel button. Instead, hold the Home button down for several seconds. This will quit the app and return you to your Home Screen.

Finding Good Apps

Finding good apps might be the biggest problem that iPad users have. With more than 140,000 apps in the App Store, it can be hard to find what you want, so here are some tips.

1. Check out the featured apps in the App Store, but be wary because they tend to be heavy on apps by large companies with well-established brands.

2. In iTunes on your computer, find an app close to what you want and then check out the Related section.

3. Look for trial versions, which often have names with "Lite" or "Free" at the end. Search for the name of the app and see if other versions turn up. Use free versions of apps to determine if it is worth paying for the full or enhanced version.

4. Tap on Ratings and Reviews.

5. Read reviews, but don't trust them completely. Casual users are not always the best at providing balanced reviews.

USING RESOURCES OUTSIDE THE APP STORE

Many good resources for finding apps aren't part of the App Store. Following are a few suggestions:

- Search using Google. For example, if you want another spreadsheet app, search "iPad App Spreadsheet."

- After you find an app that you want, try another Google search using the name of the app followed by the word "review."

- Find sites that feature and review apps. Many are out there, but be aware that some sites are paid by developers to review an app, so the review might not be the most objective.

- The author provides a list of recommended apps at http://macmost.com/featurediphoneapps.

Using iPhone/iPod touch Apps

One of the great things about using apps on the iPad is that you can use almost every app in Apple's App Store—including those originally made for the iPhone and iPod touch.

Four types of apps are in the store from an iPad-owner's perspective. A few are iPhone/iPod touch only. Avoid those, naturally. The majority are iPhone/iPod touch apps that also work on the iPad. These apps appear in the middle of the screen or scale to double the size. Some might work better than others on the iPad. You can also find apps that work only on the iPad. If you select iPad Apps from the switch at the top of a search results screen, you will see apps that are either for the iPad only, or are for both the iPhone and iPad but have been designed to use the iPad's full screen size. Otherwise, if you pick iPhone apps, you will see apps that work for both, as well as apps that work only at the iPhone screen size.

Free or Paid   App type   Sort order   Search term

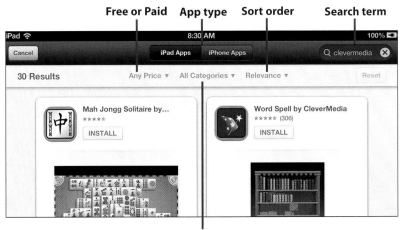

Category

For the apps that only work at the iPhone's screen size, you can scale them up so they are easier to work with on the iPad. In some cases, made-for-iPhone apps actually work better on the iPad because it is easier to see the graphics and touch the buttons.

1. To enlarge the app, tap the 2x button at the lower-right corner.

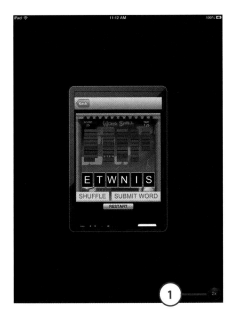

2. If the app looks blurry when it's enlarged, tap the 1x button to return to normal size.

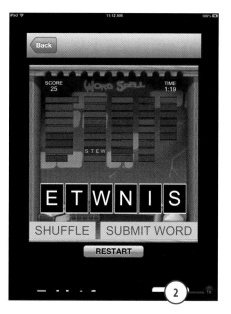

Getting Help with Apps

Apps are developed rapidly by both large and small companies. And apps are difficult to test because of Apple's restrictions on app distribution. So it is common to find bugs, have problems, or simply need to ask a question.

1. Check in the app to see if you can contact the developer. For example, in the USA Today app, an i button brings up a window for providing feedback.

2. Tap Email Support button (or a similar button in another app) to email the developer right from the app.

3. If you don't find a way to contact support in the app, launch the App Store app and search for the app there.

4. Select the app to view its information.

5. Go to the Ratings and Reviews section.

6. Tap the App Support button.

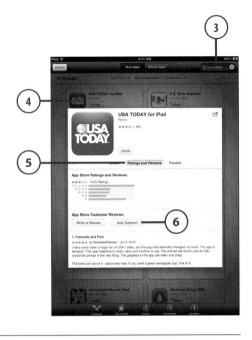

Family Sharing

When you buy an app, it can be put on any iPad (or iPhone/iPod touch if it works there, too) registered to your iTunes account. So if you share an iTunes account with your entire family, you can share your apps as well. No need to buy them again for a second iPad.

Authorizing Multiple Accounts

In iTunes on your Mac or PC, click the Store, Authorize This Computer menu item to authorize that copy of iTunes with more than one account. Then you can download apps to iTunes purchased from any of those accounts. In addition, the Home Sharing feature of iTunes lets you grab apps from one computer to another on the same network so that they can be loaded into iTunes and then synced to different iOS devices.

Keep up with news and interesting posts.

View and control your desktop computer.

Store and view documents.

Make phone calls using your iPad.

Keep up with your friends on Facebook.

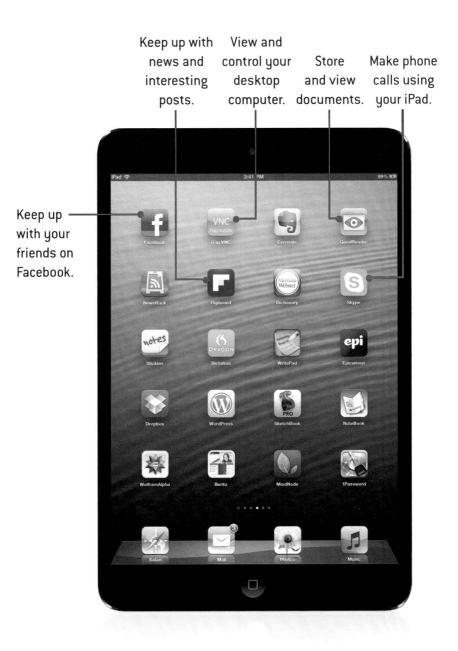

In this chapter, we take a look at various apps that you should add to your iPad to make it even more useful.

Using Popular and Critical Apps

Ask almost anyone what the best feature of the iPad is and you'll get the same answer: all the apps! The App Store is not only a source of hundreds of thousands of useful, interesting, and fun apps, but it grows each day as third-party developers and Apple add more. Here's a look at how to use some of the most popular apps for the iPad to perform various useful tasks.

Using Facebook

Many people now spend more time on Facebook than the rest of the Internet combined. If you are one of those people, the official Facebook app is probably the first third-party app you should put on your iPad.

With it you can browse your wall, post status updates, send messages, post photos, and do most things that you can do on the Facebook website, but inside an environment designed for iPad users.

1. Search the App Store for the Facebook app and install it.

2. Enter the email address you use to log into Facebook, and your password.

3. Tap Log In.

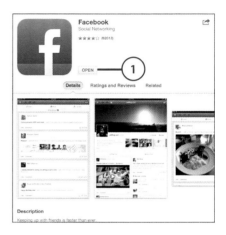

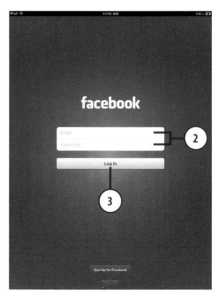

4. Scroll up and down to view your news feed.

5. Sort your feed by Top Stories or Most Recent.

6. You can Like posts just as you would on the Facebook web site.

7. You can also tap here to add a comment.

8. View and handle friend requests.

9. View direct messages and send messages to friends.

10. See your list of Facebook notifications.

11. Tap this button or swipe left to right to bring up the sidebar.

12. You can examine your own wall and edit your profile.

13. See a list of your friends and view their information and their wall.

14. You can also post to walls of Facebook pages that you manage.

15. Tap Status to update your Facebook status, adding a post to your wall.

16. Type the text of your update.

17. Add friends who you are with to the update.

18. Add a photo from your Photos library, or take a new photo using your iPad's cameras.

19. Choose groups you want to see your update.

20. Post the update to Facebook.

It All Looks Different

If there is one consistent thing about Facebook, it is change. Facebook loves to change how its website and apps look. So if the Facebook app looks different than what you see here, it could simply be that Facebook has, once again, decided to redesign the interface.

Post from Outside

With iOS 6, you don't need to use the Facebook app to post pictures. You can do it right from the Photos app and other image-handling apps. But you first need to go to the Settings app, then the Facebook section, and enter your email and password again. This gives iOS permission to use your Facebook account for posting. Then you can do things like post pictures from the Photos app, post links from Safari, and ask Siri to "update my Facebook status."

Using iTap VNC

Your iPad can be a window to your Mac or PC. By using Virtual Network Computing (VNC) technology, you can control your computer just like it was sitting in front of you (except you can't hear the sound output).

1. Search in the App Store for iTap VNC and download it. Tap the icon to launch the app.

2. On the screen that shows your current bookmarks, tap Add Manual Bookmark.

3. Enter the IP address of your computer under Host.

4. Tap Credentials and enter your ID and password for VNC access to that computer.

5. Tap Save.

Setting Up VNC on Your Computer

It takes two to VNC. You need to set up your Mac or Windows computer to accept the connection and allow your iPad to take over the screen. On a Mac, you can do this by turning on Screen Sharing in the Sharing pane of System Preferences. On Windows, it is called Remote Desktop, or you can install a third-party VNC server.

Other VNC Apps

There are many other VNC apps like iTap VNC. Also check out iTeleport for iPad, Desktop Connect, and LogMeIn Ignition. A slightly different app to look at is Air Display. It lets you use your iPad as an extra screen with your Mac or Windows PC. If you use Windows and Remote Desktop Protocol instead of VNC, there is also an iTap RDP app available.

6. After initial setup, the next time you use iTap VNC, you are prompted to select the computer from a bookmark list. Tap the name of the bookmark to establish a connection.

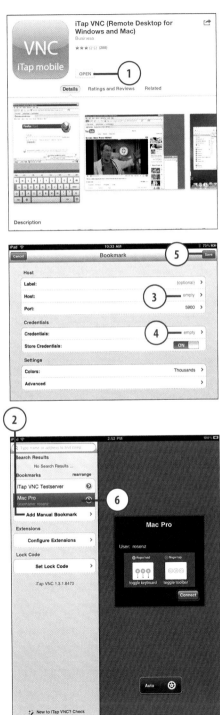

7. After you are connected, you will see a portion of your computer's screen.

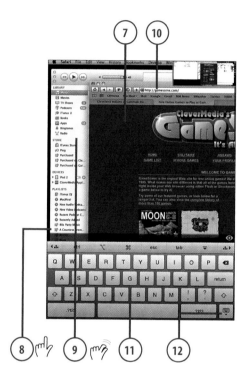

Why Won't It Work?

Getting VNC connections to work can be frustrating. It has nothing to do with the iPad. Getting them to work between a laptop and a desktop has the same difficulties. If your network router or Internet modem isn't set up just right, it won't connect and you have little indication as to why. Most of the time, VNC connections work right away, but if you are one of the unlucky few, you might need to tinker around with your network equipment settings or even call in an expert to get it to work.

8. Tap and drag to move around to see your whole screen.

9. Pinch to zoom in and out.

10. To type into an application from a keyboard, first select the application to type in by tapping, as you would click it on your computer.

11. Swipe down with three fingers on your iPad screen to open the keyboard.

12. Dismiss the keyboard with the button at the lower-right corner.

Using GoodReader

Although åiBooks is great for basic document viewing, those more serious about collecting documents to read on their iPad have looked to apps that have even more features. Apps such as GoodReader enable you to create a library of viewable files such as PDFs, Word, images, text, and so on. You can then access these documents any time.

1. Search the App Store for GoodReader and add it to your apps.

2. On the left side of GoodReader's main screen, you see the documents you have on your iPad.

3. On the right side are various controls. For instance, you can browse the web or enter a URL to download a document from the web.

4. You can also see Internet locations you have set up access to, such as your Dropbox account.

5. Tap Add to add more Internet services.

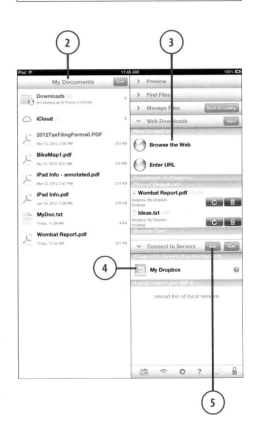

6. You can access your documents stored in Google Docs.

7. You can use Dropbox or one of the other major cloud file storage services.

8. You can use a standard Internet sharing service, such as FTP.

9. You can also access Macs using standard file sharing.

10. Tap a document to open it.

11. Documents of all different types, such as PDF, Pages, Word, text, images, and audio files can be viewed.

12. Documents open in tabs, allowing you to switch easily between several documents.

13. You can use annotation tools to mark up the document.

14. You can search the document and use various reading tools. If the document is editable, such as a text document, then you can also use editing tools here.

15. Tap to return to your list of documents and services.

Transfer via iTunes

You can also transfer files between your Mac or PC and your iPad into GoodReader when you sync, without using any special Internet services or setting up file sharing. See "Syncing Documents" in Chapter 3.

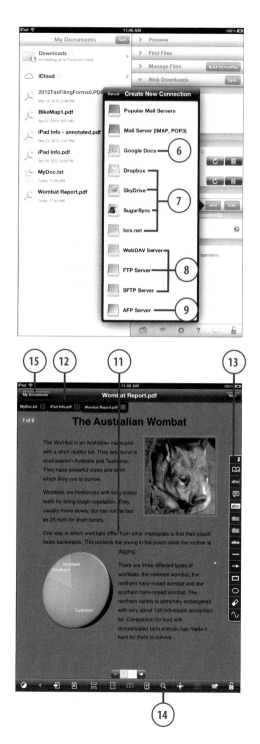

Using NewsRack

If you read a lot of online news and blogs, you probably use RSS from time to time to view these sources as feeds, rather than visiting the website. NewsRack is one RSS feed reader for the iPad.

1. Search the App Store for NewsRack and add it to your apps. After it has been installed, launch NewsRack.

2. Tap Add Feeds. (Or use Sync Settings to sync your Google Reader settings.)

3. Tap the Add Feed button. This will look very different in horizontal screen orientation, so keep it vertical for now.

4. In the Enter Feed URL field, enter the domain name for a website.

5. Tap Show Feeds. A list of RSS feeds from the site will appear.

Finding RSS Feeds

RSS feeds are everywhere. Chances are your local newspaper and your favorite blogs and online magazines all have RSS feeds. Try the URL for any website in NewsRack and see what feeds are available.

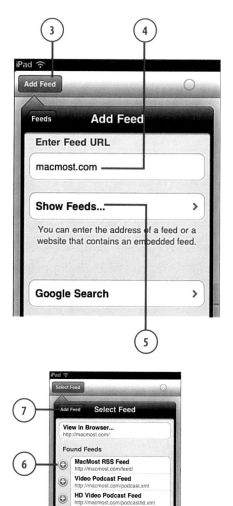

6. Tap the + button to the left of any feed you want to subscribe to.

7. Tap the back menu button (labeled Add Feed on this example) until you get a Done button, so you can complete the action of adding feeds.

Lots of RSS Reader Apps

Since the iPad is an ideal device for reading the news, many RSS reader apps have appeared. Other popular ones include Pulse News Reader, NetNewsWire, GoReader Pro, and Reeder for iPad. Search in the App Store for "rss reader," and you will come up with even more.

8. Tap Feeds at the top to look at a list of all your RSS feeds.

9. Tap Unread to view all the unread items in all your feeds.

   Alternatively, tap a single feed to just see that feed.

10. Tap the Edit button to add more feeds or delete existing feeds.

11. You see a mix of all the unread items in all your feeds. Tap any one to read it.

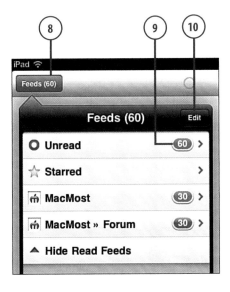

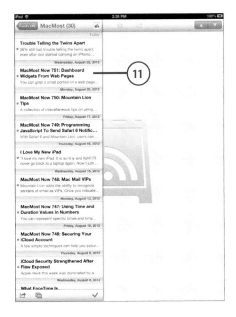

MAKE THE IPAD YOUR NEW NEWSPAPER

No need to get a physical paper dropped on your doorstep anymore. Many major newspapers and magazines deliver via their iPad apps. Look for apps from *USA Today*, the *New York Times*, the *Wall Street Journal*, *Newsweek*, *Time*, and *Wired*. There is even an iPad-only newspaper called *The Daily*. You can even create your own newspaper using multiple sources with the app The Early Edition.

In some cases, the app and the daily content are free. Sometimes you need to pay for the app, but the content is free. Other times, such as with magazines, you pay for each issue you download. For newspapers like *The Daily*, you can sign up for a weekly subscription fee.

Newspapers that don't have a custom app can still be viewed in the iPad's web browser, often with more up-to-date content than you can get with a paper edition.

Using Flipboard

How about a magazine that is all about you? Well, at least about your friends and things that you like. Such a thing exists, called Flipboard. It uses information from your Facebook, Twitter, and other social media accounts to show news stories, pictures, and posts from your friends. It also uses your RSS feeds to show you news you are interested in. To see page after page of things that should interest you, just keep flipping.

1. Search for Flipboard in the App Store. Then install it and launch it.

2. The front page contains featured Flipboard stories that change every few seconds. Tap on the image to read more.

3. Swipe the Flip button to the left to continue to your main Flipboard page.

4. Sections match either a subject or a social network that you have added to your Flipboard.

5. Tap a section to view stories in it.

6. Swipe to move to the next page of sections.

7. Tap a story to view the original text and images.

8. Flip to the next page to view more stories.

9. Return to the sections page.

10. Tap the red tag to view which social networks and sites make up your Flipboard content.

11. These are the sources you have set up so far.

12. Add more social networks and sources.

13. Add some popular news sources by category.

14. Search for news sources using keywords.

Adding a Dictionary

It would be a crime to have to carry a dictionary with you in addition to your iPad. Of course, the solution is to get a dictionary app for your iPad. The Merriam-Webster Dictionary HD app is a free download from the App Store. There is also a premium version that removes the ads and adds illustrations and other features for a few dollars.

1. Find the Merriam-Webster Dictionary HD app in the App Store, install it, and then launch it.

Use Any Online Dictionary

Of course, if you prefer another dictionary that doesn't have an iPad app, you can always just bookmark that site in Safari. You can also create a Home screen bookmark as we did in Chapter 7.

2. Tap in the search box and enter a word to look up.

3. You can also tap the microphone button and speak the word to look it up. Handy if you don't know how to spell the word.

4. The word and definition appears.

5. You can tap here to have the word spoken so you can hear its pronunciation.

6. The app can also be used as a thesaurus. A list of synonyms appears at the bottom. Tap any one to jump to that word. In fact, any blue word in the definition can also be tapped to jump to that word for further clarification.

Using Skype for iPad

Your iPad works quite well as a phone when you use a VoIP (voice over IP) app. Skype is probably the most well known. Make sure you get Skype for iPad and not the small-screen iPhone Skype app.

1. Search for Skype in the App Store. Make sure you look for the iPad app, not the iPhone/iPod touch app of the same name. Install it and then launch it.

2. When you run the Skype app, you need to enter your ID and password and then sign in. After you do this the first time, you can skip this screen.

Get a Skype Account

You need a Skype account to use the Skype app. You can get a free one at http://www.skype.com/. If you find the service useful, you might want to upgrade to a paid account, which lets you call land lines and other phones. The free account lets you call only other Skype users.

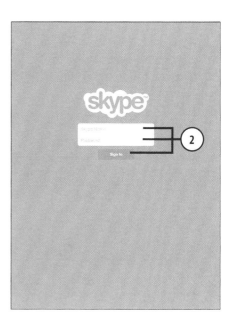

3. Use the on-screen keypad to enter a phone number. You need a country code, too, which means using a 1 for U.S. calls. It should be there by default.

4. Tap Call.

5. While placing a call, you see the status, and eventually the elapsed time, and Mute and Hold buttons.

6. Tap the hang up button to hang up.

How Do You Hold Your iPad to Talk?

The microphone is at the top of your iPad. The speaker is at the bottom on the back. The best way may be to just put the iPad in front of you and ignore the locations of both. Or, you can get a set of iPhone earbuds.

How About Skype Video?

You can also make video calls with Skype using your iPad's cameras. But you must be connecting to another Skype user who also has a video camera connected to their computer, or perhaps they are using an iPad as well.

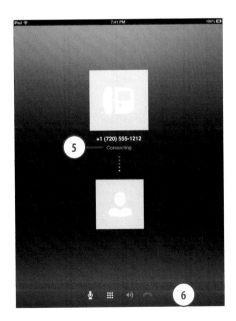

Putting Notes on Your Home/Lock Screen

Your Lock screen and Home screen backgrounds look pretty. But can they be functional? One app attempts to make them more useful by enabling you to put sticky notes on them. Search in the App Store for Stick It and add it to your collection of apps.

1. Search for Sticky Notes HD in the App Store. Install it and then launch it.

2. Tap + to create a new note. You may be asked to choose Small or Large. Choose Large.

3. Select a color from the list. You can also select different note types, such as talk bubbles, pieces of paper, or even just plain text boxes.

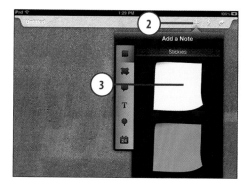

4. Type a note using the on-screen keyboard.

5. Tap Done.

6. Drag the note into a better position.

7. Tap the bottom-left corner to pick a background image.

8. Choose a background from the Library, Colors, or Photos buttons. Tap a new background.

9. Tap Done.

10. Tap the Export button.

11. Tap Save to Camera Roll.

12. Tap Dismiss.

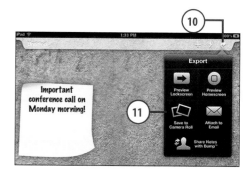

The App Can't Do It for You

Although the Stick It app is great for making backgrounds with notes on them, it can't make these backgrounds your Lock or Home screen. You have to do that yourself using the Photos app or the Brightness & Wallpaper settings in the Settings app.

13. Press your Home button to return to the Home screen and then tap the Photos icon.

14. Find the photo you just took and tap it.

15. Tap the Boxed Arrow button.

16. Tap Use as Wallpaper.

17. Tap Set Lock Screen.

18. Press the Wake/Sleep Button at the top of your iPad.

19. Press the Home button.

20. The background, complete with the sticky note, now appears on your Lock screen.

Emergency Contact Info

Another use for this app is to quickly and easily put your emergency contact information on the Lock screen. You can just put a "In case of emergency" phone number and instructions on the screen, or "If found, please call:" phone number.

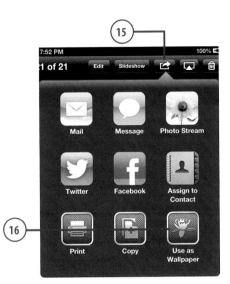

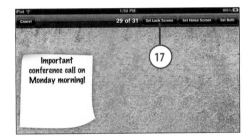

Creating Multimedia Cloud Notes with Evernote

One of the most popular productivity apps on the iPad and iPhone, as well as Macs and PCs, is Evernote. At its heart, it is like the built-in Notes app on your iPad. You can create text notes, and they will sync across your devices.

But Evernote has several advanced features that endear it to users. First, you can easily record audio and take photos and add them to your notes. Second, it is independent of an email service like iCloud or Gmail. Third, there are Evernote clients for almost every computer and device. You can even view your notes in a web-based interface if you need to.

1. Search for Evernote in the App Store and install it.

2. If you have never used Evernote, you can create a new account on your iPad. Basic accounts are free.

3. If you already have an Evernote account, just enter your ID and password to log on.

4. The main screen will show your notes. Tap a note to view it.

5. To create a new note, tap here.

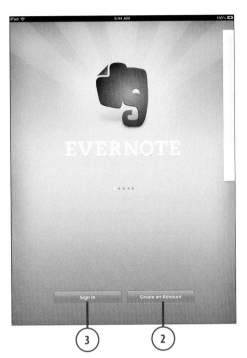

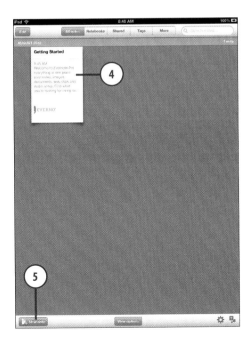

6. Tap in the title area to type a name for the note.

7. Tap in the body area to type text into the note.

8. At any time you can tap the photo button to take a picture with your iPad and add it to the note at the current cursor location. The button next to it allows you to select a photo from your photo library.

9. Tap Evernote's microphone button to record a voice memo or simply record the sound around you.

10. You can format text with a variety of controls, even creating check-boxes and lists.

11. Tap the info button to get info on a note.

12. You can add tags to notes as one way to organize them.

13. If you allow it, notes will include location information about where you were when you created the note.

14. You can share the note on Face-book, Twitter, via Email, or print it.

15. You can search the content of notes.

The real power of Evernote involves how it syncs quickly and wirelessly over the Internet. For instance, you can use it to write notes, record audio, and take pictures with your iPad while out of the office, and then find them all on your Mac or PC when you get back to your desk. Often, the picture-taking ability is used to grab snapshots of sketches on napkins or product infor-mation on the back of a box.

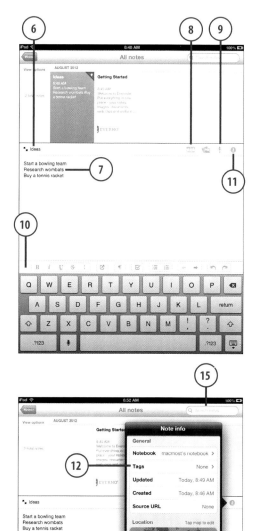

You Want Audio While Taking Notes?

If you want to record audio and take notes at the same time, try the app SoundNote. You can tap out text with the keyboard and draw with your finger all while audio is being recorded. Then it remembers where the audio stream was for each word. So tap a word to hear the audio at that moment.

Another app that does this is Circus Ponies NoteBook. You can type text, draw, take photos, and so on. You can turn on audio recording, and then each line in your note will match up with a portion of a recording. So you can sit in a lecture or meeting and take notes, and then refer back to the audio that matches each portion of your note. Wish I had these back in college!

Handwriting Notes

You'd think with a touch screen that the iPad could recognize your handwriting instead of making you type on an on-screen keyboard. The WritePad app enables you to take notes by typing or by using the touch screen to write with your finger.

1. Find WritePad in the App Store. Install it and launch it.

2. Tap the My Documents button to view your current documents.

3. Tap + to start a new document.

4. You can create folders to organize your documents if you want.

5. Tap and drag around the screen using the tip of your finger like a pen or pencil. Start in the upper-left corner. You can use printed letters, cursive, or a mixture.

6. Stop writing and wait for the text to process. When it does, the text appears at the cursor location.

7. Tap the buttons at the top-right corner to switch between Reading mode, Writing mode, and Keyboard mode.

8. Tap the Undo button to undo the last text processed.

Looking for a Different Handwriting App?

If you'd rather have an excellent app that just lets you write and draw on the screen, try Penultimate. You create notebooks and write in them by drawing with your finger. You can also mark up PDF documents and enter text using the on-screen keyboard.

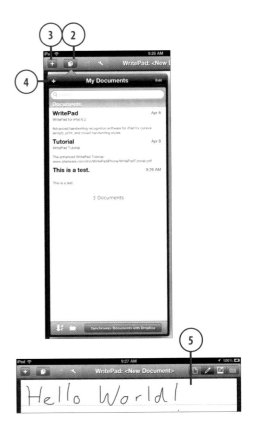

Using Epicurious

One application for early personal computers was to store and recall recipes. With the Internet, we can also share those recipes. And now with the iPad, there is finally a way to easily have these recipes with you in the kitchen while cooking. The Epicurious app is a favorite for such tasks.

1. Search for Epicurious in the App Store. Download and launch.

2. Tap the Control Panel to see a list of featured sections.

3. Use the search box to search for a recipe.

4. Tap a section.

5. Tap a recipe.

6. You'll get a list of ingredients needed.

7. You can then follow the recipe. If only cooking were that easy! Bon Appetit!

Other Useful Apps

So many useful apps are in the store that it is impossible to cover them all in a book. Here are some quick mentions of others you can check out. Some are free, others you have to pay for.

- **SketchBook Pro**: This drawing app lets you paint with your fingers. Professional artists have used it to create some amazing pieces. There is even a Flickr gallery of SketchBook pro art. You should also check out **Brushes**, **ArtStudio**, and the free **Adobe Ideas** app.

- **1Password**: Mac users already know about the popular 1Password for Mac. The iPad version doesn't integrate with Safari, but it does give you a place to securely store passwords and other important information.

- **Things**: If you are into productivity apps and to-do lists, check out Things. It is the king of to-do list apps on the iPad. Also check out **Wunderlist**.

- **Bento 4 for iPad**: If you need to create databases, check out Bento. It is a powerful database tool that you can use for serious business purposes, or just to keep track of the DVDs you own.

- **MindNode**: If you use mind mapping software to organize your ideas and plan projects, then you'll be happy to know there is a pretty advanced tool that lets you do this on the iPad.

- **OmniGraffle**: If you need to create organizational charts, or like to use graphics to plan out projects, check out the iPad version of this popular graphics tool.

- **WordPress**: The official WordPress app lets you write, edit, and maintain your blog posts. It works for the WordPress.com blogging service and for WordPress blogs set up on independent sites.

- **StarWalk**: This is a must-have app for anyone even vaguely interested in astronomy. Even if you aren't, the beautiful, up-to-the-minute renderings of the night sky on your iPad will impress your friends. You can see what the sky looks like right now, right where you are, and use it as a guide to identifying what you see. Also check out **The Elements: A Visual Exploration** for more cool science learning.

- **Wolfram Alpha**: Want to compare two stocks, see the molecular structure of sulfuric acid, or calculate the amount of sodium in your breakfast?

Would you believe that one app does all three and has hundreds of other interesting answers to all sorts of questions? It is also the answer engine behind a lot of what the iPhone's Siri feature does, so you get a little bit of Siri on your iPad.

- **USA Today**: While other national newspapers are playing around with pay-to-read models, *USA Today* is sticking with free. It provides a great summary of what is going on around the country. If you are looking for a more European perspective, the **BBC News** app also provides news, plus a lot of video.

- **The Weather Channel Max+**: If you get your news on your iPad, you might as well get the weather, too. This free app covers it all, with maps, forecasts, current conditions, and even video. But there are plenty of other weather apps in the store, too. Check out **Weather HD** in particular.

Compose music.

Stream movies and TV shows.

Read comics.

Listen to music.

Play games.

Track your best scores and challenge friends.

In this chapter, we look at apps that exist for entertainment purposes such as viewing movies, reading comics, listening to music, or playing games.

Games and Entertainment

You can view a lot of information and get a lot of work done on the iPad, but it is still a great device for entertainment. The majority of entertainment apps out there are games, but there are also some general entertainment apps that we can take a look at.

Composing Music with GarageBand

It is hard to sum up GarageBand in just a few pages. This little brother to the Mac GarageBand application is a very big app. It could almost deserve a book all to itself. Let's look at how to create a simple song.

1. Purchase and install GarageBand from the App Store. Launch it from the home screen. See "Purchasing an App," in Chapter 15 for instructions on how to find and download apps.

2. If this is the first time you are using GarageBand, you can skip to step 3. Otherwise, you will see a list of songs you have created. Tap the + button and then New Song.

3. Now you can choose an instrument to start. Select the keyboard.

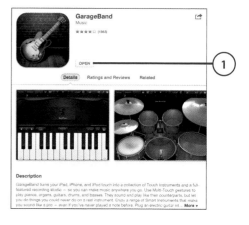

4. Tap the keys to play notes. The force at which you hit the keys and the spot on the key determines the exact sound it produces.

5. Tap the instrument button and swipe left or right to change from Grand Piano to one of dozens of other instruments.

6. Tap the record button to record what you are playing. A metronome will count down, so wait one measure before starting. Try just a few notes, only one or two measures.

7. Tap the Stop button when you are done recording.

8. Tap the Undo button if you didn't quite get the notes right. Then try again.

9. After you have recorded a bit of music, the View button will appear. You can use that to switch to the Tracks view.

10. In Tracks view, you will see the bit of music you recorded. Tap on it once to select it. Tap again to bring up a menu that includes Cut, Copy, Delete, Loop, Split, and Edit. Tap Loop.

11. The music you recorded is now set to loop for the entire section of the song. Tap the Play button to test it.

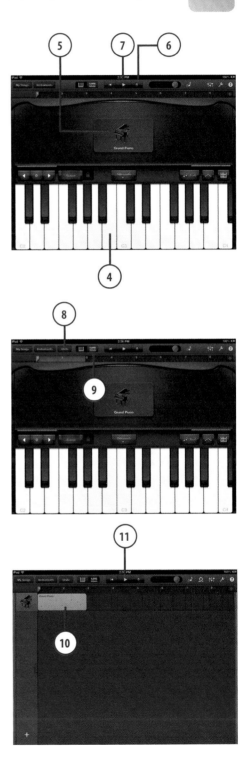

12. Tap the Loop button to view pre-made loops that you can add to your song.

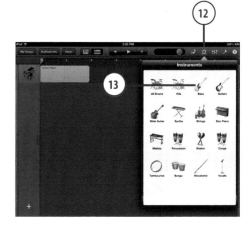

13. Tap an instrument to select the type of loop you want to add.

14. You can filter the list of loops by Instrument, Genre, or keyword Descriptors.

15. Select a loop to test it. You can even have your loop playing at the same time by tapping the Play button at the top and then tapping a loop from the Apple Loops menu to see how they sound together.

16. Drag a loop from the list to the area right under the loop you created.

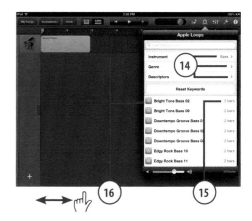

17. Now you have your original loop and a drum loop. Tap play to hear them together.

You can continue to add loops. Add a bass line and maybe some guitar. You can also double-tap on the left side of each track where you see the image of the instrument, to return to the instrument view and switch instruments or record more notes.

Besides the piano, you can also play guitar, bass, or drums. And each instrument has several variations. Plus, there are smart instruments, such as the smart guitar, that only allow you to play notes and chords that fit well together.

See http://macmost.com/ipadguide/ for more tutorials on using GarageBand for iPad.

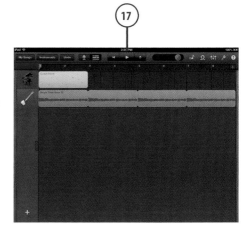

Watching Movies and TV Shows with Netflix

Netflix started as a DVD rental service using mail rather than retail stores, but it is quickly changing into an online video rental service. One of the first acclaimed apps for the iPad was the Netflix app. Netflix subscribers can use it to rent and watch movies right on their iPads.

1. Enter your email address and password, and then tap Sign In. If you don't have an account, you can actually sign up for a trial account right on your iPad.

2. Tap an image to start streaming the video.

3. Tap the information next to an image to find out more about the video.

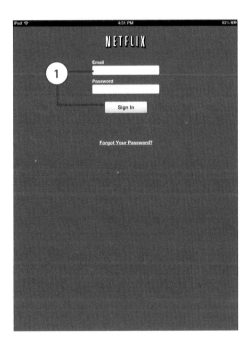

4. In this case, the video is actually a TV series, so another screen appears with a list of episodes. Tap an episode to watch it.

5. The movie should start after a few seconds. You have Play and Pause controls at the bottom of the screen.

6. After the video starts playing, the controls will disappear. To bring up the controls again, tap in the center of the screen. You can double-tap in the center of the screen to enlarge the video, or just turn your iPad sideways for a better view.

7. Use the large slider at the bottom to jump around in the movie.

8. Tap the Done button to return to the previous screen.

You Have to Be Online

Although watching movies in the Netflix app is unlimited, you can't download and store the movie for later viewing. You need to be online to watch. iTunes rentals, on the other hand, can be stored and watched while offline, like on an airplane flight.

More Streaming Video

Netflix is not the only main choice for streaming video. Another app called Amazon Instant Video gives you access to similar content with lots of movies and TV shows. Instead of subscribing to Netflix, you can subscribe to Amazon's service through your Amazon.com account.

Hulu, another service that streams TV shows and movies, also has an iPad app called Hulu Plus. It works with the same Hulu account that you may already be using to view shows on the Hulu website.

Listening to Music with Pandora Radio

The Music app isn't the only way to listen to music on your iPad. In addition to the many streaming Internet radio station apps, there is Pandora, which enables you to make your own radio station based on a song or artist.

1. Search for Pandora in the App Store and install it.

2. When you first run Pandora, you can choose to use your existing account or create a new one, and then you will be prompted for some additional information.

3. When you are past the sign in/sign up stage, you see your stations to the left. To create a new station, tap in the field at the upper-left corner. Type in a name.

4. Pandora creates the new station and starts playing a song. If you like the song and think it represents what you want for this station, tap the Thumbs Up button.

5. If you think this isn't a song that should be played on this station, tap the Thumbs Down button.

6. Tap the Skip button if you think the song fits, but just don't want to hear it at the moment.

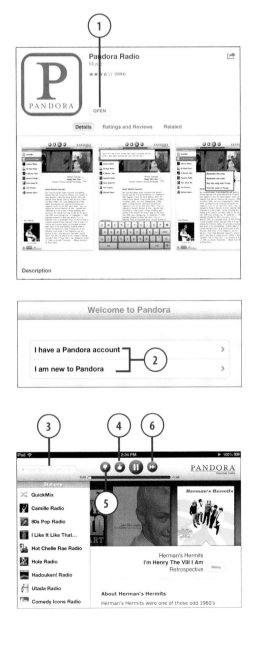

Pandora Everywhere

The stations you create on the iPad also show up in your Pandora account wherever you log on. You can use Pandora on your computer by just going to http://www.pandora.com/ and logging in. You can also use Pandora on many mobile phones. There are even television sets and car radios that play your Pandora radio stations.

Spotify Too

Another way to listen to music without iTunes is to use the Spotify app. Unlike Pandora, you can search for and play specific artists, albums, and songs. A Spotify subscription gets you access to its entire library, which includes most of the music recorded in the last few decades. The iPad app even lets you download music while you have a Wi-Fi connection so you can listen to it later when you don't.

Using Game Center

Apple has created a single unified system for high scores, achievements, and multiplayer gameplay. A large portion of the best games in the App Store have adopted this system, called Game Center.

Your game center account is the same one you use to purchase apps in the App Store. After you use the Game Center app to log in, you won't have to log in directly in any of the games. It all works seamlessly.

1. Tap the Game Center app to launch it. The app comes with your iPad.

2. Enter your Apple ID and password and Sign In.

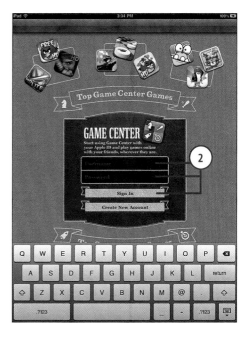

3. You'll see the number of games you have that connect to Game Center, plus the number of achievements you have accomplished in the game.

4. Tap Friends to see a list of people you have connected with in Game Center. You can challenge them to play a game.

5. Tap Games to see your scores and achievements for each game.

6. In the list of games, you can see your high scores. Tap a game to get more details.

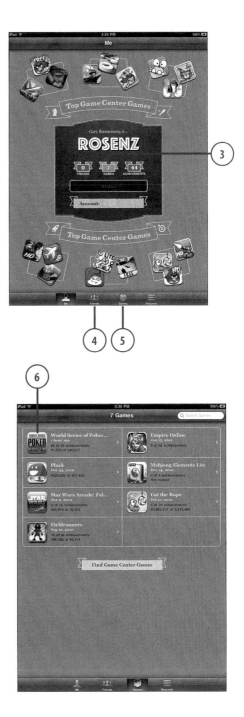

7. You can view a list of the world's best scores and see how you compare. Tap Achievements to see which ones you have and which you are missing.

You can often also see high scores and achievements inside the games themselves, even though they are stored in the Game Center system. You can challenge friends to games or to beat your scores from inside some games.

iPad Games and Entertainment

Even if you purchased your iPad to stay connected, get work done, or watch videos, you might want to check out the rich and wonderful world of games.

With the touch screen and accelerometer control, the iPhone and iPod touch turned out to be fertile ground for game developers. Add to that the large screen and fast processor of the iPad and you have a powerful and unique gaming device.

Let's take a look at some of the best games for the iPad.

Air Hockey

At first glance, this game looks simple. You control a paddle by moving your finger across the screen. You can play against a computer opponent that is actually quite challenging.

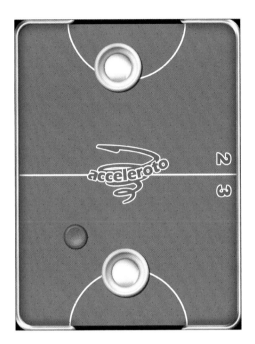

What's special is the ability to play against a second player at the other end of your iPad. Just set it down on a table and play head-to-head. This is made possible by the multitouch screen. The iPad needs to keep track of two fingers on the iPad. And it does it very smoothly.

Highborn HD

Do you like strategy and adventure? Highborn HD is a turn-based strategy game that takes you through a story of fantasy and magic. You deploy various units through short scenarios to conquer the board or achieve goals.

The thing that sets Highborn apart from other turn-based strategy games is a deep sense of humor. It helps you through the unavoidable tutorial and even makes you read all of the unit descriptions.

Harbor Master HD

One of the new game genres that appeared on the iPhone was the draw-to-direct type of game. It first appeared with a game called Flight Control, which is also available on the iPad.

Harbor Master HD takes the genre a little further. The idea is you direct ships into docks by drawing with your finger. Simply draw a line from the ship to the dock and the ship follows the path.

The game gets harder as you go along, with more and more ships unloading cargo and then sailing away. You have to make sure the ships find a dock and that they never collide.

Angry Birds HD

Many people purchase games to play on an iPad. But some people buy an iPad to play a game. When that is the case, the game responsible is usually Angry Birds HD.

In this game, you shoot birds at a structure using a slingshot. Your goal is to destroy the pigs living in the building. Sounds a bit strange, but behind the premise is a good physics simulation that presents challenges with every level. And it has also spawned some sequels, like Angry Birds Seasons HD and Angry Birds Space HD.

Galcon Fusion

Galcon was a huge hit on the iPhone, and all the time you couldn't help but wonder how much better it would be on a larger touch screen. Now we know, because we have Galcon Fusion for the iPad.

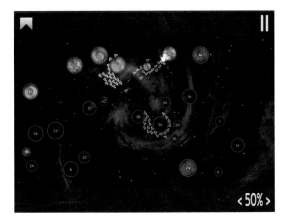

In this game, you conquer a small cluster of planets using ships. The game looks like a strategy game, and you must use strategy to win. But it plays like an arcade game because all you do is tap and drag to send ships from one planet to another.

Plants vs. Zombies HD

Zombies are attacking your house, and you need to defend it. So, what do you use? Strange mutant fighting plants, of course.

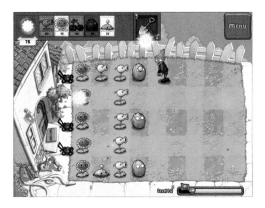

It sounds weird, and it is. But as a fun strategy game, it works. It plays like a tower-defense style game but with fun elements that you find in those $20 PC game downloads.

Monkey Island 2 Special Edition

If you played this game back when it was first a hit on the PC, then you'll be excited to know that it has been re-imagined for the iPad. It is the same adventure, but with beautiful graphics and sound.

If you have never heard of Monkey Island, then you really shouldn't wait any longer. This game probably represents the pinnacle of computer adventure games and can give you hours of head-scratching and gut-busting fun.

Scrabble for iPad

My favorite game on the iPhone was Scrabble. The same game comes to the iPad but with some special new features. Not only can you play against a tough computer opponent, a friend on Facebook, or your local network, but you can also play against a friend in the same room, using your iPhones.

You just both download the Tile Rack app for the iPhone and then use the iPad as the main game board; your tiles appear only on your iPhones.

Fieldrunners for iPad

A major genre of touch device gaming is tower defense. In these games, you build walls and armaments to defend against a never-ending onslaught of enemy troops. Probably the best in this group is Fieldrunners.

The enemies come out of specific spots at the sides of the board and try to move across it. You have to gun them down before they reach the other side. But you are on a budget. So, choose your weapons and place them carefully.

Real Racing 2 HD

A much more advanced use of accelerometers is when you use them to steer a car while racing. There are many racing games for the iPhone, and some have already made their way over to the iPad.

Real Racing HD is one that has excellent graphics and game play. It also has lots of options, including a career mode, car choices, and so on. It is close to some console racing games in features and graphics.

Gold Strike

I'll go ahead and mention two of my own games here. Gold Strike was first a web-based game, then a PC game, and then an iPhone game. Once you try it, you'll see that it was really an iPad game all along, just waiting for the iPad to come along.

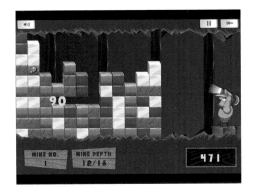

You tap groups of blocks to remove them before the mine fills up. Gold blocks give you points, and the larger the group, the more points you get. The iPad version also includes some game variations for extended play.

Word Spy

Word Spy is a word search game where you look for groups of letters that form a word. The longer the word, the more points you receive. Each level requires that you get a certain number of points before you can continue.

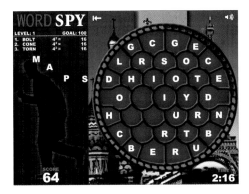

For a real challenge, the Intercept game variation is where you look for cities and code words hidden in the pattern of letters. Both Gold Strike and Word Spy are examples of popular web-based games that have made a transition to the iPad.

Comics

The iPad is a great platform for reading comics. The Comics app (sometimes called Comics+) is one of the many comic book apps that enable you to purchase and read comics. It has some of the best graphic quality, and you can even download some free comics to try it out.

There are dozens of other quality comics in the App Store. Some comics even have their own app. Look for the Marvel Comics app, the Comics app, DC Comics, IDW Comics, Comic Zeal, and others. Most apps that allow you to download various issues are free and charge you on a per-issue basis.

Subscribing to Magazines with Newsstand

A special app that comes with your iPad is really an app folder with a special purpose. This folder is the Newsstand. It looks like a set of bookshelves with magazines on it, assuming you have populated it with some publications.

When you install a magazine app, it will usually go into your Newsstand folder automatically. The developer of the app has to submit the app to Apple as a newsstand app in order for this to happen, so you may find that some apps behave just like normal apps, and won't go into Newsstand.

1. Tap the Newsstand icon to open up the folder of magazine apps.

2. Tap a magazine to run the app. What you find when you run the app depends on the app developer. You will usually find a list of issues you have downloaded, more issues that you can download for free or purchase, and often the ability to "subscribe" so that you pay once and get a year or more of issues.

3. Tap Store to go to the App Store. This is basically a shortcut to the Newsstand section of the App Store. You can also get to it by launching the App Store app and going to this section.

4. Tap outside of the Newsstand folder to close it.

Already a Subscriber?

Some magazines offer the iPad version for free to those who get the print edition of the magazine. When you launch the app, you might see a button or feature that allows you to enter a code from the mailing label on your magazine, and it uses that to verify you are a subscriber. Then, the downloads are free.

Often the iPad version of the magazine has interactive features like videos, music, and clickable areas on the page. So it is worth it to get it on your iPad, even if the print copy is lying on your coffee table.

Zinio

While some magazines have their own apps, many others can be found inside the app called Zinio. It is kind of a clearinghouse for hundreds of magazines that publish with a standard format. Browse sample articles for free, and then look for magazines you can purchase either as a single issue or as a subscription. You can even get European and Asian magazines that are hard to find in the U.S.

Extend your iPad mini with printers, cases, connectors, and keyboards.

In this chapter, we use some optional accessories like cases, docks, keyboards, and adapters.

→ Printing from Your iPad mini
→ iPad mini Smart Cover
→ Power Accessories and Docks
→ Video Output Adapters
→ Apple Wireless Keyboard
→ Protecting Your iPad mini
→ SD Card and USB Adapters

iPad mini Accessories

Many accessories available for your iPad mini perform a variety of tasks, protect it, or just make it look pretty.

You might already have some things that work with your iPad mini—printers and wireless keyboards, for instance. Let's look at a variety of accessories to see how to use them.

Printing from Your iPad mini

Some time after the release of the first iPad, Apple added wireless printing to the iOS operating system. They call it AirPrint. You can print a web page or document directly from your iPad over your wireless network.

The one catch? It works only with newer printers that support AirPrint. Fortunately, the list is growing fast and now includes printers by many companies. You can find an updated list of AirPrint printers at http://support. apple.com/kb/ht4356.

Assuming you have one of these printers and have set it up on your local network, here's how you print, using the Pages app as an example.

1. In Pages, with the document you want to print open, tap the Tools button.

2. Tap Share and Print.

3. Tap Print.

4. If you have never used this particular printer before, you'll need to
add it to the iPad's list of printers.
Tap Select Printer.

5. If the printer is on and has been
configured to your network, it
should appear in a list. Tap it to
select it.

6. The printer will now appear in the
button.

7. Tap Range to specify a range of
pages to print, or leave it at All
Pages. The Range option will
appear only if you have more than
one page in your document.

8. Tap here to set the number of
copies to print, or leave it at 1
Copy.

9. Tap the Print button to send to
the printer.

At this point, your iPad will launch
a special Printer Center app. You
may not notice it unless you
quickly double-press the Home
button to bring up the Recents
List. You will then see this Print
Center app running.

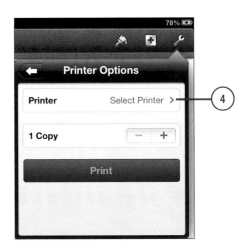

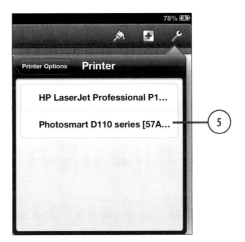

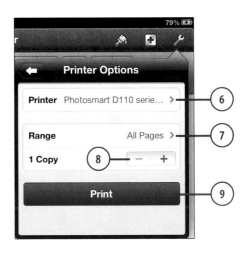

10. Double-press the Home button to bring up the Recents List.

11. Tap the Print Center icon to bring up a status menu.

12. You can see the status of the printing process and other information.

13. Tap Cancel Printing to stop printing.

Different for Other Apps

How you initiate printing differs from app to app. Using Safari, for example, you go to the same button at the top of the screen that you use for book-marking a page. You see Print as one of the options. In the Photos app, it is the same button that enables you to email a photo, among other things.

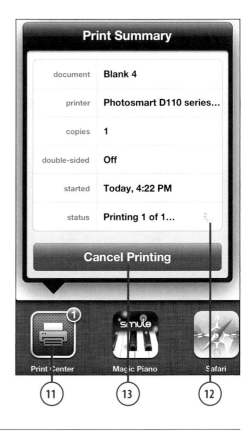

Bypassing Apple's AirPrint

Although not all Wi-Fi printers support AirPrint, there is a way to cheat. Some enterprising third-party developers have come up with software for Macs that sets up a printer connected to the Mac as an AirPrint printer. You aren't really printing directly to a printer—you are going through the Mac. Still, it may be a good option for some. Search on the web for the Macintosh software Printopia, FingerPrint, or AirPrint Activator.

iPad mini Smart Cover

A cover is just a cover, right? But Apple didn't make "just a cover" for the iPad mini. They made a "smart cover." By using magnets, this cover sticks to the front of the iPad mini without hiding the rest of the iPad's design. And it is highly functional, acting as a stand as well.

1. The cover will align to the front of your iPad using magnets and protect the screen.

2. Unfold the cover and two things will happen: the lining will clean your screen slightly, and the iPad will automatically wake up from sleep.

(Courtesy of Apple Inc.)

3. Fold the cover all the way back to form a triangle and elevate one side of the iPad for typing.

4. Flip the iPad over, and it will lean against the triangle-configured cover to stand the iPad up for watching video or using FaceTime.

(Courtesy of Apple Inc.)

It Comes in Colors

You can get the Smart Cover in six colors. Plus, with the magnets built into the iPad, there are sure to be third-party case makers that come out with even more styles in the future.

(Courtesy of Apple Inc.)

Power Accessories and Docks

A power user of any gadget usually acquires additional power chargers and cables. For instance, you might want to charge your iPad at home and at work. Remembering to carry the adapter with you everywhere you go usually doesn't work out well because it is too easy to forget.

You can buy a second charger and dock cable from Apple that is the equivalent of the one that came with your iPad and even pipe the audio into external speakers through the dock.

Here is a list of items you might want to consider:

- **Apple iPad 12W USB power adapter**: A 12-watt adapter that charges the iPad at full speed, faster than a standard USB port. You'll need to also get an extra Lighting to USB connector to connect it to your iPad. Otherwise, you could use the one that came with your iPad mini as long as you remember to bring it along. But most people who buy a second charger will also want to get a second cable to go along with it.

- **Apple Lightning to USB cable**: If you just want an extra dock cable to plug your iPad into a Mac or PC for syncing and slow charging. Many cars and some public places like airports now have USB outlets that you can use with this cable or the one that came with your iPad. It is always good to have a spare cable, as losing your only one means you can't charge your iPad.

- **Car Charger**: If you want to charge your iPad in your car, get a car charger. You can find several: The Griffin PowerJolt Car Charger, the Kensington PowerBolt Micro Car Charger, and the Incase Car Charger. Incase also makes a "combo" charger that works from both AC power and cars. Make sure the charger you buy matches the Lightning connector on the bottom of your iPad mini. However, many chargers simply use a USB connector, allowing you to plug in either cable type provided you have your own Lightning cable.

Incase Mini Car Charger

Not All Power Is the Same

Your iPad requires extra power to charge properly. With the power supply that came with your iPad, a 10 or 12 watt model, it should charge fully after about 4 hours. But with an iPhone power supply, or while hooked up to a full-power USB port on a computer, it takes twice that amount of time since those are 6 watts. Some low-power USB ports on computers won't charge the iPad at all.

Video Output Adapters

If you want to show your iPad mini's screen, or output video or a presentation from your iPad, you need to use either a cable or an Apple TV. Apple sells several dock adapters that send video from the dock to a monitor, television, or projector.

Lightning to VGA Adapter

The Lightning to VGA Adapter attaches on one end to the dock port on the bottom of your iPad. The other end is a VGA port you attach to a VGA cable that can be attached to a monitor or projector.

Whereas the original iPad could show only movies, presentations, and slide-shows, the iPad mini can use this adapter to show almost anything that is on the screen.

1. Connect the Lightning to VGA adapter to the dock port on your iPad.

2. Connect the other end of the adapter to a standard VGA cable.

3. Connect the other end of the VGA cable to a monitor or projector that accepts a VGA connection.

4. Use an audio mini jack to connect the headphone port of the iPad to the line in on the projector. The exact type of cable you need depends on what audio input the project takes.

(Courtesy of Apple Inc.)

5. At this point, the video on the projector or monitor should mirror that of the iPad. Some apps may show different things on the iPad's screen and the external display. For example, Keynote will show the presentation on the external display, while you have the presentation plus controls on the iPad's screen.

Lightning Digital AV Adapter

This is an HDMI connector that enables you to connect directly to televisions and newer projectors that have an HDMI port. In addition, you can connect HDMI and another dock cable at the same time, allowing you to keep your iPad charged.

(Courtesy of Apple Inc.)

An HDMI connection gives you a higher quality connection over a VGA adapter. But while most modern televisions have HDMI input, it is still rare on school and corporate projectors. The way you use an HDMI adapter is the same as how you use a VGA one. It will mirror the screen except in cases like with Keynote.

TV Compatibility

The video coming from the iPad is compatible with both 720p and 1080p HD televisions and video devices. It also includes audio over the HDMI cable. Many televisions support only 1080i, not 1080p. In that case, the video may be shown in 720p instead.

AirPlay Mirroring with Apple TV

The second generation Apple TV, the one that looks like a little black box, may be the best iPad accessory of them all. It enables you to mirror the screen of the iPad just like the VGA and HDMI cables do. But you can do this wirelessly, using the local Wi-Fi network and something called AirPlay mirroring.

You need to make sure several things are in place before you can use AirPlay Mirroring.

1. Make sure that both your iPad and Apple TV are connected to the same local network.

2. Make sure both your iPad and Apple TV are up-to-date. Using older or mismatched versions of software on the devices could prevent AirPlay from working.

3. Turn on AirPlay on your Apple TV. To do this, go into Settings, AirPlay, and turn it on.

4. On your iPad, double-tap the Home button to bring up the Recents list at the bottom of the screen.

(Courtesy of Apple Inc.)

5. Swipe left to right to get to the media controls.

6. Tap the AirPlay button.

7. Select which Apple TV you want to mirror the iPad's screen.

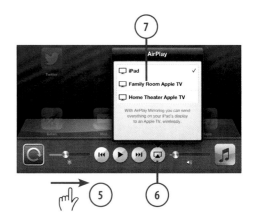

To stop AirPlay mirroring, just repeat steps 4 through 7, selecting the iPad instead of one of the Apple TVs.

The $99 for an Apple TV may be worth it just as an AirPlay accessory for the iPad. But you also get all the other Apple TV features, such as iTunes movie rentals, YouTube, Netflix and Hulu apps, and streaming for iTunes on Macs and PCs.

The Mirror Crack'd

You'll notice that some apps won't mirror to Apple TV at all. Certain video streaming apps have purposely restricted mirroring due to licensing issues and other reasons. So you might not be able to mirror when using apps from certain cable networks.

Apple Wireless Keyboard

If you have a lot of typing to do, and are sitting at a desk anyway, you can use Apple's Bluetooth keyboard with your iPad mini. This is the same wireless keyboard that you would use with a Mac.

1. To connect to the Apple Wireless Keyboard, first make sure that you have good batteries in it.

Choosing the Right Wireless Keyboard

If you have an older Apple wireless keyboard, it might not work with your iPad. The Apple Store warns that only "newer" keyboards can successfully connect to the iPad. Reports from people with older wireless keyboards indicate that this is true. However, you don't need to stick with Apple's wireless keyboard. Most Bluetooth keyboards work fine with the iPad. Search your favorite online store for all kinds of compact wireless Bluetooth keyboards. Check reviews to see if anyone has mentioned trying the model with an iPad.

(Courtesy of Apple Inc.)

2. Go to the Settings app on your iPad and tap on the General settings on the left.

3. Tap Bluetooth to go to the Bluetooth settings.

4. Make sure Bluetooth is turned on. Switch it on if not.

5. Turn on your Apple Wireless Keyboard by pressing the button on its right side. You should see a small green light turn on at the upper-right corner of the main face of the keyboard.

6. After a second or two, the keyboard should appear on your iPad screen. Tap where you see Not Paired on the iPad screen.

7. Look for a 4-digit number in the message displayed. Type that on your keyboard. Then press the Return key.

8. After the connection is established, you should see Connected next to the name of your keyboard.

9. After you connect, the iPad automatically uses the physical keyboard by default, rather than bringing up the on-screen keyboard. To use the on-screen keyboard again, you can either disconnect or power off your Apple Wireless Keyboard, or you can press the Eject button at the upper-right corner of the keyboard to switch to the on-screen keyboard at any time.

SPECIAL KEYS

The Apple wireless keyboard was not made for the iPad—it existed first. But the iPad recognizes many special keys on it and uses those keys in various ways.

- Brightness (F1 and F2): Changes the brightness of the iPad screen

- Volume (F10, F11, and F12): Mutes, lowers, and raises the volume

- Eject (To the right of F12): Brings up or dismisses the on-screen keyboard

- Arrows: Navigates around in editable text

- Arrows+Shift: Selects editable text

- Command: Can be used with X, C, and V for cut, copy, and paste inside editable text

- Audio Playback Keys (F7, F8, and F9): Goes to previous track, play/pause, and next track

Size Matters

Remember that each version of the iPad is physically different. The original iPad and the iPad 2 are different shapes. The 3rd and 4th generation are slightly larger than the iPad 2. The 4th generation has a different dock type on the bottom. Of course the iPad mini is much smaller than all of them. Check the product carefully to make sure you are getting one that fits your device.

SD Card and USB Adapters

Apple sells two adapters that can be used to connect your camera to your iPad mini. The first is a Lighting to SD Card Camera Reader that lets you take an SD card and connect it to your iPad. The second is the Lightning to USB Camera Adapter that lets you plug your camera and other devices directly into your iPad.

Here is how to import photos directly from your camera or SD card.

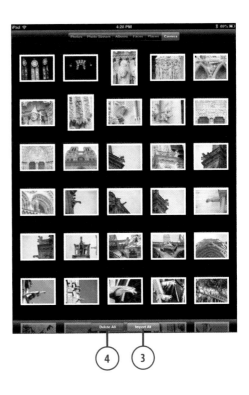

1. Connect either the USB Camera Adapter connector or the SD Card Camera Reader to your iPad's dock port.

2. Connect your camera using the USB cable that came with it, or slide the SD card into the card reader. If you are connecting a camera, you will most likely need to switch the camera on and into the same mode you use to transfer pictures to a computer.

3. After a slight delay, the Photos app should launch and images on the camera or card should appear on your iPad's screen. Tap Import All to import all the photos on the card.

4. Tap the Delete All button if you want to delete the images without ever importing them into your iPad.

5. If you don't want to import or delete all of the images, tap one or more images to select them.

6. Tap Import.

7. Tap Import Selected to bring in only the selected photos.

8. After importing the photos, you will be given the change to delete them from the camera or card. Tap Delete to remove them.

9. Tap Keep to leave the images on the camera or card.

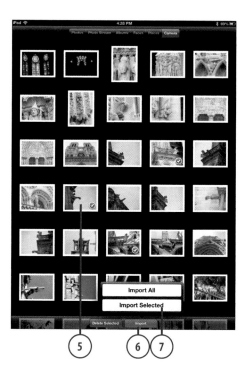

More Than Just Cameras!

The Lightning to USB Camera Adapter does a lot more than just let you use cameras and SD cards. You can also connect USB headsets with it and use them as headphones and/or a microphone. You can connect low-power USB keyboards as well. The SD card reader can be used to transfer video and images, so you can use it to play stored movies from SD cards.

Wirelessly Transfer from Camera to iPad

With the Eye-Fi card (www.eye.fi) you can take pictures with your digital camera and wirelessly transfer them from your camera to your iPad. You can even do this while you are taking more pictures. The card is something you install in your camera that acts like a regular SD card, but it also contains a tiny wireless transmitter. Then you use a free iPad app to connect the card to your iPad. Snap a picture and it appears on your iPad.

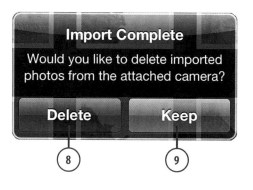

Index

CHECK OUT MUST-HAVE BOOKS IN THE BESTSELLING MY... SERIES

| ISBN-13: 9780789750334 | ISBN-13: 9780789748515 | ISBN-13: 9780789749895 | ISBN-13: 9780789749819 |

Full-Color, Step-by-Step Guides

The My... series is a visually rich, task-based series to help you get up and running with your new device and technology and tap into some of the hidden, or less obvious features. The organized, task-based format allows you to quickly and easily find exactly the task you want to accomplish, and then shows you how to achieve it with minimal text and plenty of visual cues.

Visit quepublishing.com/mybooks to learn more about the My... book series from Que.

Your purchase of *My iPad® mini* includes access to a free online edition for 45 days through the **Safari Books Online** subscription service. Nearly every Que book is available online through **Safari Books Online**, along with thousands of books and videos from publishers such as Addison-Wesley Professional, Cisco Press, Exam Cram, IBM Press, O'Reilly Media, Prentice Hall, Sams, and VMware Press.

Safari Books Online is a digital library providing searchable, on-demand access to thousands of technology, digital media, and professional development books and videos from leading publishers. With one monthly or yearly subscription price, you get unlimited access to learning tools and information on topics including mobile app and software development, tips and tricks on using your favorite gadgets, networking, project management, graphic design, and much more.

Activate your FREE Online Edition at
informit.com/safarifree

STEP 1:   Enter the coupon code: UGNANXA.

STEP 2:   New Safari users, complete the brief registration form.
Safari subscribers, just log in.

If you have difficulty registering on Safari or accessing the online edition,
please e-mail customer-service@safaribooksonline.com